SMART PARENTING
FOR AFRICAN AMERICANS

SMART PARENTING FOR AFRICAN AMERICANS

Helping Your Kids Thrive
in a Difficult World

Jeffrey Gardere, Ph.D.

A Citadel Press Book
Published by Carol Publishing Group

To my children,
Puma-Xavier and Q'vanaa Elektra,
My reasons for living.
I love you very much!

A Citadel Press Book
Published by Carol Publishing Group
Citadel Press is a registered trademark of Carol Communications, Inc.

Editorial, sales and distribution, rights and permissions inquiries should be
addressed to Carol Publishing Group, 120 Enterprise Avenue, Secaucus, N.J. 07094.

In Canada: Canadian Manda Group, One Atlantic Avenue, Suite 105, Toronto,
Ontario M6K 3E7

Carol Publishing Group books may be purchased in bulk at special discounts for
sales promotion, fund-raising, or educational purposes. Special editions can be
created to specifications. For details, contact Special Sales Department, Carol
Publishing Group, 120 Enterprise Avenue, Secaucus, N.J. 07094.

Manufactured in the United States of America
10 9 8 7 6 5 4 3 2 1

Library of Congress Cataloging-in-Publication Data

Gardere, Jeffrey Roger.
    Smart parenting for African Americans: helping your kids thrive
in a difficult world / Jeffrey Gardere.
        p.   cm.
    "A Citadel Press book."
    ISBN 0–8065–2051–5 (pbk.)
    1. Parenting—United States.   2. Parent and child—United States.
3. Afro-American children—Conduct of life.   4. Afro-American
children—Life Skills guides.   5. Afro-American families—
Psychology.   6. Self-esteem in children—United States.
7. Prejudices in children—United States.   I. Title.
HQ755.85.G366   1999
649'.1—dc21   98–55217
                                                                        CIP

CONTENTS

PREFACE

Smart Parenting for African Americans has been written to be a lifelong guide to all parents who want professional and commonsense advice on how to prepare and empower their kids to successfully navigate and grow from the experiences and realities of the world, both good and bad. This book operates under the basic premise that prejudice and institutional racism is an added stress that children of color must recognize and face as they grow and mature, every single day of their lives. Thus, much of the advice provided in *Smart Parenting* incorporates strategies that help address and resolve day-to-day challenges, as well as situations with racism and prejudice at their foundations.

At the same time, it is not my intention to lament or complain about racism and prejudice; nor do I consider them excuses for antisocial, rebellious, or defeatist behavior. They are simply presented as sociological and psychological factors, along with typical maturation issues, which influence the emotional and physical state of black children.

Although I am both a clinician and social scientist, I have deliberately steered clear of presenting a scientifically based book steeped in research, where every opinion must be substantiated by some study. I find much of this type of information to be boring mumbo jumbo, and frankly, most of it does not pertain to African-American children. On the other hand, most of the advice and opinions I have presented in *Smart*

Parenting are based on my day-to-day experiences as a clinical psychologist who has treated thousands of black and Hispanic families from all socioeconomic levels. I fancy myself a Freudian-trained clinician whose real education came from the streets and ghettos of the world. Therefore, the advice provided here is a hybrid of both "street" and clinical expertise. In other words, I've kept it "real."

You will notice that my grammar and written voice are very informal at times. Although I do not encourage my children or yours to speak in this type of slang, there is a method to my madness. First, this is how many of our children talk, and I want you to get the flavor and understanding of the intensity and complexities of their existence. If you cannot demonstrate a grasp of their language, it becomes very easy for them to set up emotional barriers against you, their parents. Finally, to be honest, I have been immersed so deeply into our "generation next" that their slang has become my own. What can I say? Kids are at the cutting edge of what's cool!

Why do we need a parenting book specifically for African Americans? The fact of the matter is that society is not color-blind. Our global society has different standards in the way it treats and perceives people of color, resulting in economic and educational disparities. It is these disparities that place black children at risk for failure and dangers of every kind. I also realized that through my talk-show appearances, especially on *The New Maury Povich Show, The Ricki Lake Show,* and *The Montel Williams Show,* I had developed a strong following among all races, and an even stronger following among young black people and their parents. This was partly because of the way I dressed—my earring, my ponytail (which is now gone)—and partly because of the way I was able to communicate in a straightforward but compassionate manner with the studio guests and audience members. So in more ways than one you could say that I was the obvious choice to do a black-parenting book. In fact, this book was the perfect vehicle for passing on my expertise and continued experiences with generation next. The Lord does work in mysterious ways!

I must admit that writing this book has been one of the hardest things I've ever done in my life. After years of giving advice on television and the radio, often speaking off the top of my head or giving sound bytes, I had to really spell out the advice in a way that made sense to every parent reading the book. But the effort has been so worthwhile!

Smart Parenting for African Americans is a needed book that has come at the right time. Black parents, rich, poor, and in between, are at their wit's end trying to figure out their kids and raise them right. It really does seem like our kids are rejecting all of the things that we as parents have worked so hard to achieve—especially an improved but still racist society. I expect that as this book answers many questions and offers good, constructive advice, there will be more of a demand and curiosity to find options and solutions to raising black children to succeed.

Due to time constraints, I initially did not want to write *Smart Parenting for African Americans*, but it now appears to be a book that should have been written a long time ago. I am proud to have been chosen by my publishers, and especially by God, to be the author of this book which I hope will touch many lives in a very positive manner. Unlike the many self-help books out there, which promise to help you fix your life in ten minutes or less, or find a husband in forty-two hours, *Smart Parenting* does not present grand illusions. This book is not a gimmick. Instead, it allows me to be your private psychologist, personal resource, coach, partner, and adviser in assisting you in one of the most impossible jobs in the world, parenting.

You'll hear me say it many times: Parenting is a work in progress, and *Smart Parenting* will help guide you to successful parenting every step of the way, from before the birth of your child, right through those excruciating teen years. From failing grades to failing attitudes and identity crises, from the dangers of sexual predators to the threat of being harassed by rouge cops, from the negative influence of hip-hop and teen rebellion to the realities of developing sexuality and much more, *Smart Parenting* offers expert and commonsense advice on how to get inside the mind and world of your children so you can develop better insight into the problems they face. With *Smart Parenting*, you'll find that the information and simple strategies provided will immediately translate to more open communication and a trusting relationship with your child and teenager. The knowledge gained from this book will help you develop the parenting skills to successfully empower and raise confident, intelligent, and spiritually strong black children who will take on and conquer all of life's adversities.

ACKNOWLEDGMENTS

First and foremost, I would like to thank God for blessing me with the opportunity to share my knowledge and professional experiences in order to help African-American parents and children to a better and more productive life.

I am particularly grateful to my editor, Carrie Cantor, who was taskmaster, English professor, and cheerleader throughout this process. Carrie, I apologize for any gray hairs I caused you, but what we have created together is for the good of others, and for that I hope it was worth it.

I am also grateful to my wife, Deyanira, who gave me permission to work on the book almost every weeknight and weekend, even though it took time away from being a husband; Puma and Q'vanaa, for letting daddy work on the book and playing quietly—I know it's tough for a four- and a six-year old to understand the meaning of the word *deadline*; my sister Barbara, who put up with my foul moods when I was getting stressed over the book; Ed Lucaire, and Janus Adams for giving advice and sharing their experiences a writers; as well my heartfelt gratitude to Nikita Pitts for proofreading many of the chapters; Marsha Goldsburry and Virginia Cangelo for their continued prayers; and Angela Collins, my friend and supporter. I hope I don't let any of you down.

INTRODUCTION: BUILDING SELF-ESTEEM— THE ESSENTIAL TASK OF SMART PARENTING

Self-esteem is a deep-seated confidence in oneself and one's abilities that allows a person to face and conquer life's challenges. Children with high self-esteem have the confidence to succeed in school because they believe they are intelligent. They participate in sports and the arts because they know they are talented. They dare to dream and turn those dreams into realities because they know they can. They don't do hard drugs because they love and value themselves too highly to be self-destructive.

But where does this self-esteem come from? Why, it largely comes from you, the parents. It comes from the way you love, regard, and speak to your children, who will learn to believe in themselves if you believe in them. They will develop self-esteem if you support and encourage their abilities and efforts at meeting life's challenges—big ones, little ones, and all those in between.

What about the child who has low self-esteem? This child loses the race every time because he never leaves the starting gate. He does not have the confidence or the belief in his own abilities to even try. He feels stupid, incompetent, and unworthy. Why? Because he is used to hearing that he is stupid, lazy, or bad. Quite often he hears this from his parents when they are angry and feel stupid themselves (probably because their own parents told them *they* were stupid). He will eventually internalize negative statements that he continually hears from his parents, like "I am stupid," "I always make mommy angry," "I can't do well in school," and "I'm a bad boy." These are powerful and destructive beliefs that our children absorb from the earliest ages, resulting in a chronic lack of self-esteem.

This lack of self-esteem becomes the main ingredient to a life of fear, failure, and self-hate. If you don't believe in your child, he will have a hard time believing in himself. Therefore, your most important job as a parent, and an essential ingredient of smart parenting, is to positively affect your child's self-esteem. What you say has a tremendous impact on your child's self-image. You are the most important person in your child's life, and he will depend on you to impart good feelings and nurturing every minute of the day. That is why it is important to promote and protect your child's self-esteem by showing unconditional love and acceptance, not denigration and humiliation. For example, it's one thing to be angry at something your child has done and address that issue. It's another to lose your temper and attack your child by calling him lazy or stupid.

Because of your importance in your child's eyes, the things you say leave a remarkable impression on his self-image. Smart parenting means telling your child every day, "You are just as beautiful and intelligent as anyone else in this world." Smart parenting means that you encourage and shower praise on your child for even the slightest achievement because the pride the child feels will spur him on to even greater achievements. Smart parenting means that even when you feel irritable and annoyed at your child for not knowing how to do something, you refrain from showing that irritation and making your child feel incompetent. Instead, you show forgiveness and understanding and encourage him to start again, and, with your guidance and encouragement, do it right. For example, if your child is trying to tie her shoe and can't, you don't just do it for her—you encourage her efforts and assure her that she will eventually be able to do it. With smart parenting, you will let your child know that you will always be there as a support, a cheerleader, a rock. With this kind of back-up, your child will develop the self-esteem to take on life and win.

Self-Esteem in a Prejudiced Society

Good self-esteem is a quintessential part of a solid personality, especially in light of the social and psychological challenges that your young child will face within the first few years of life while growing up black in America.

Television   Our society is hooked on television. It is a source of entertainment, information, and education. Statistics show that young children spend an average of four hours a day in front of the television. It stands to reason that their self-image and understanding of the world is heavily influenced by their TV watching. If your black child watches television, he will be bombarded with images of, on the one hand, successful and beautiful whites and, on the other hand, mainly struggling and less attractive blacks. Eventually, he will begin to think that blacks must not be as smart as whites, blacks are not as attractive as whites, and therefore he, as a black person, is inferior to whites. This becomes a serious impediment to developing self-esteem and a positive self-image.

School   Our schools are doing the best they can to help educate children and build character. There are some impediments to these efforts, especially in public schools, which the majority of black children attend. They include poor funding, dilapidated buildings, classroom overcrowding, and crime. The burden of these problems is often felt by teachers who become overwhelmed and sometimes hopeless. They, in turn, take this frustration out on the kids by having little patience with them. Some teachers lose control and in various ways impart to the kids that they have little ability or are stupid. This is devastating to the developing self-esteem of all children, especially black children.

Being a Minority in a White World   Another serious challenge to self-esteem is the reality of being a minority with second class status in a majority (white world). Growing up in a multicultural society, your child will have white peers who will inadvertently and unintentionally communicate their "superiority" and your child's "inferiority." Their superiority will be exhibited by the private camps they attend or the houses in which they live, or even what their parents do for a living. Even though your child may have some of those material advantages, he will also see that many black kids don't have the same social position. The knowledge that so many white kids do have it and black kids don't have will most certainly affect his self-esteem.

As a child, I also suffered from lack of self-esteem but for slightly different reasons. Growing up in the 1960s I was one of the first black children in the Catholic grade school I attended. Receiving a Eurocentric education, in which all the heroes were white and the achievements of blacks were no more than footnotes in our textbooks, I always felt less intelligent than my peers, despite the fact I never carried less than an A– average. And my classmates were no help. In their misguided efforts to show acceptance they would often say, "Oh, Jeff, he's okay. He's one of the 'good ones'." So I'm thinking, if I'm one of the "good ones," I must be an anomaly from inferior stock. Therefore, how good can I really be? I believe that what got me through this make-or-break stage of life was the fact that my parents believed in me and let me know it.

That's the point in a nutshell. Helping your black child build self-esteem from day one of her life will give her the strength and intestinal fortitude to be ambitious, adventuresome, curious, and assertive. In addition, she will be able to successfully meet and beat the situations that challenge young black children. Whether the challenge is having to deal with negative media images, being part of a defective educational system or even being exposed to overt and malicious racism, the child with self-esteem has the best chance to avoid becoming just another statistic. She will be more than just a survivor; she will be a victor!

SMART PARENTING
FOR AFRICAN AMERICANS

1

IT'S NEVER TOO SOON
TO GET SMART

THE OLD SAYING "An ounce of prevention is worth a pound of cure" has never been so true as when it comes to smart parenting. From building your child's self-esteem, right through to encouraging self-confidence and self-discipline, smart parenting during the very early childhood years will provide the most positive results in your child. Though it is never too late in your child's life to begin smart parenting, he will have an even stronger emotional foundation when traits such as self-esteem and self-worth are taught as early as possible.

How important is early childhood parenting? Quite simply, it provides the difference between a healthy, bright, self-assured child and one who constantly struggles and eventually loses out to the ever present challenges of life. In other words, it separates the winners from the losers. On which side would you like your child to be? Through effective early parenting, you can help your child go for the gold. You, that's right, *you* have the power and responsibility to not only model positive parenting behavior but also to educate and guide your child to become a healthy individual in all aspects of functioning.

Smart Parenting Before Birth

If you want to build strong and powerful character traits in your child, I cannot stress enough that you must begin active

3

nurturing as early as possible in your child's life, even during pregnancy. The earlier you start providing love, a healthy positive home, and constant support and pride, the more influence you will have on your child's development. I am also thoroughly convinced that smart and early parenting may be the best way to minimize the physical and emotional toll that life's challenges and adversities take on youngsters. The key is laying the groundwork well and early.

If you happen to be planning to have a child or are expecting one now, you are in the best position to think about and employ early parenting, which is the first step in *smart* parenting. Though nothing in life is guaranteed, good prenatal care drastically increases the odds of giving birth to a healthy baby. This good health in turn provides the building blocks for developing proper emotional and intellectual growth.

The Effects of Drugs, Alcohol, and Tobacco on a Fetus

If you are interested or responsible enough to be reading this book, chances are you already know about the dangers of smoking, drinking, and drugging to the health of the unborn child. Yet some of you may think that drinking wine with dinner, smoking pot on weekends, or even the occasional cigarette won't really hurt your unborn baby. Some may even indulge more than occasionally but don't think you have a problem. But you do have a problem, and so will your unborn child. The fact is that even occasional use of these substances is hazardous to the health of your child.

What do I mean by hazardous? How about low birth weight and birth defects such as missing limbs, asthma, or an oversized head? Drugs and alcohol also negatively affect the brain development of the fetus, resulting in a host of physiological and intellectual deficits such as conduct disorders, learning disabilities, a low I.Q., and even mental retardation. Any way you paint it, it's not a pretty picture. That's reality! If you do not want the heartache of watching your child struggle and live with a disability or chronic illness, especially one caused by your carelessness, then you must follow Dr. Jeff's orders. Take personal stock and a hard look at your life. If you've been living anything less than a healthy lifestyle, now is the time to change, for yourself *and* your child.

Proper Nutrition and Exercise

Beyond eliminating destructive behaviors, there's also a lot more you can do to improve yourself and protect your unborn child's health. Let's take the issue of proper nutrition. I once promoted a wellness program for women of color on a popular New York radio call-in show. I discussed the issue of obesity and how it is endemic to the black community—sometimes soul food can just be too darn tasty! I also discussed the importance of nutrition and exercise in maintaining appropriate body weight. I thought I was doing a public service, but then I received many angry calls from black women who thought I was pushing a white woman's ethic of beauty.

In many ways I can understand how they feel. Many black women are struggling to love themselves and build their self-esteem, which means accepting themselves, even if their bodies are less than perfect. Second, being overweight is often reinforced in black society by many men who love their women PHAT—plenty of hips and chest. Unfortunately, this adoration reinforces a disregard for good nutrition and fitness.

The fact of the matter is that poor nutrition results not only in obesity and myriad health problems—even worse, it harms the unborn child. It is now accepted and common knowledge that good nutrition during pregnancy benefits the health of both the mother and the unborn baby. Women who eat well and avoid known risks tend to have fewer complications during pregnancy and labor—and they deliver larger, healthier babies. Full-term babies that weigh seven pounds or more tend to have higher I.Q.s and fewer physical problems than full-term babies weighing less than five-and-a-half pounds.

If you happen to be overweight, put off dieting until after your baby is born. Instead, concentrate on moderate exercise and on improving the quality of the food you eat. Soul food is not only delicious, it actually can be good for you too, if you can find ways to prepare the food healthfully. (Check out Wilbert Jones's *The Healthy Soul-Food Cookbook*, Birch Lane Press, 1998.)

Sisters, when it comes to your unborn baby, let's bury the argument of what physical beauty really is. Smart parenting dictates that you've got to eat right. In addition, you've got to exercise and stay in shape to increase the chances of having a healthier baby. Again, consult with your OB/GYN or family doctor for an appropriate diet and exercise plan. If you already exercise, then continue and adapt your routine to suit your changing body. Not only will exercise help you and your baby stay healthy, exercising while pregnant will put you more in touch with your body and all that's happening during this strange and wonderful experience. Exercise keeps both the heart and body healthy and fit, preventing backaches, improving posture, and promoting early recovery after delivery.

Certain guidelines need to be followed for proper exercise during pregnancy. The American College of Obstetrics and Gynecology recommends the following:

- Drink plenty of water during and after exercise to regulate your baby's body temperature and your own.
- Don't exercise to the point of physical exhaustion.
- If you start feeling pain, exhaustion, or dizziness during exercise, stop right away.
- Avoid exercise in the supine, or back-lying, position after the first three months of pregnancy.
- Eat more to compensate for the additional calories needed for exercise and healthy pregnancy.
- Regular exercise, at least three times a week, is much more preferable to working out only once in a while.

There are many exercise and nutrition books that can safely guide you during pregnancy. Here are a few that are well worth the effort of reading:

Tupler, Judith and Thompson, Andrea. *Maternity Fitness: Preparing for Healthy Pregnancy.* New York: Simon and Schuster, 1996.

Eisenberg, Arlene and Eisenberg, Sandy. *What to Eat When You're Expecting.* New York: Workman Press, 1986.

Johnson, Robert. *Mayo Clinic Complete Book of Pregnancy in Baby's First Year.* New York: William Morrow, 1994.

Hess, Mary Abbott and Hunt, Anne. *Eating for Two: The*

Complete Guide to Nutrition During Pregnancy. New York: MacMillan, 1992.

By the way, exercise doesn't have to be complicated, and you don't have to spend a mint on some health club, either. You could simply take quick-paced walks to get your legs and heart going. Walking is a great activity for couples to do together, encouraging the equal responsibility of parenting and togetherness.

Yoga as Exercise and a Stress Reducer

Another inexpensive and great form of exercise while you are pregnant is yoga. Yoga is not only good exercise, it also incorporates breathing and stress reduction, which enhances your emotional well-being and that of your child's, as well as makes the birthing process easier.

Try a yoga class specifically for pregnant women, which is also an excellent way to meet other women who are expecting and with whom you can share your experience. Being able to share stories about struggles and the fun times with others who are in the same position is incredibly powerful, especially since pregnancy can sometimes feel like a very lonely affair.

Whether in a class or on your own, I strongly recommend establishing a morning and evening routine of yogalike practices meant to reduce the stress of pregnancy and increase the emotional calm of your unborn child. You can experiment a bit to create a routine that best suits your particular needs and likes, but here are a few suggestions:

- Upon waking, instead of jumping up and starting your day, take a few minutes to practice deep, relaxing breathing. They can be simple, deep breaths or a more formal meditation. Combine this with the gentle rubbing of your belly. It's helpful if your partner joins you. This will create a greater bond between the two of you as parents, and with your child. Deep breathing will relax you and the baby, easing you into the day. You will find that you are less irritable and better able to deal with stress. During the day, repeat this whenever possible, even if it's only for a minute at a time.

- During your deep breathing, conjure up positive images of yourself and your child. Envision your child floating happily inside of you. Picture him born and being held by you. These images will be soothing and promote good feelings that will make you feel more relaxed. In turn, this will provide a very calming atmosphere for the baby. All of these practices will put you in a more positive frame of mind and, if continued, can help you manage the stresses you will face once your child has arrived. (An excellent book is *Yoga for Pregnancy: Safe and Gentle Stretches*, by Sandra Jordan, St. Martin's, 1998).

Prenatal Education

Your child can hear from within the womb, and can certainly hear your voice throughout the day as you speak. Another practice I recommend during the morning routine, and especially before you go to sleep in the evening, is talking to your child. Both parents should do this. It is very relaxing for the unborn baby. You can also read to your child from books you will also read after birth. If there are other children in the family, they should also try to communicate and read to the unborn child. This exercise can certainly be a bonding ritual for everyone in the family, but just as important, this type of prenatal stimulation may also be helpful for the future intelligence of your baby.

I am a true believer in prenatal education and have espoused its use to all the expectant parents whom I have worked with in therapy. Though this is a controversial topic that has many disbelievers, there is a slew of scientific studies that show that babies can begin to process information from the outside world by the seventh day of conception. More recent studies promote prenatal stimulation even more fervently by recommending stimulation through parenting activities such as reading to the fetus, which is viewed as being vitally important, and even necessary for the growing brain to continue its development.

I also believe and recommend playing music as a stress reducer for mom, and a stress reducer and a source of education for the baby to come. Again, if prenatal reading can enhance intelligence, it stands to reason that exposure to music in the womb will also positively influence future intellectual skills. Although this idea may have been somewhat controversial ten years ago, most researchers believe there is a causal link between prenatal music stimulation and the enhancement of some kind of intelligence and creativity during and after the birth of the child. Researcher Peter G. Hepper, reporting in the *Irish Journal of Psychology* (1991), studied fetuses two to four days old that had been exposed to the tune of a popular TV program while their mothers were pregnant. When the same tune was presented after birth, the babies exhibited changes in heart rate and movements. The results seem to indicate that learning can happen *before* birth—but it doesn't end there. There are other benefits to the child receiving both prenatal and after-birth music stimulation and education. Other researchers showed a causal relationship between exposure to music and abstract post-birth reasoning ability. They believe that music has many benefits for children beyond those within the arena of music itself. Music is thought to contribute to the development of intellectual, motor, and social abilities and skills. In other words, a child who becomes proficient in music has a greater possibility of also being proficient in nonrelated musical skills.

What does all this work to relax and bring a sense of well-being mean to the mother and the unborn baby? Perhaps nothing. But experience has shown me time and time again that well-adjusted, happy, intelligent children don't get that way by accident. It is instead a natural progression, starting with the earliest positive experiences inside the womb and continuing on to the outside world and daily life. So, once again, my professional opinion? Try it—you have nothing to lose and everything to gain!

Preparing the Environment

A lot of what we've talked about so far in this chapter has had to do with mom (with dad as a support) taking care of herself and baby through good nutrition; the elimination of drugs, tobacco, and alcohol; exercise; and relaxation techniques, which include yoga, reading, and music. Of course, the point of all of these activities is to strengthen the host body (mom) so that the fetus has a healthy and stimulating environment in the womb, increasing the chances of a healthy birth and a child strong in body, mind, and spirit.

What about the environment called home, in essence, an extension of the mother's womb, where the child will grow and live with parents, family, and friends? The home is not only the foundation of love and belonging, but also the shelter from the storm, the locale where one develops the courage and strength to venture out into the world. During the early years of life, this most important place will nurture the infant's personality and help build character. By the same token, this environment, if not properly created and structured, can destroy the psychological potential and self-esteem of even the most emotionally resilient child.

As parents, it is within our power to put together a home environment that will not only nurture but also bring out the best in our children, especially during infancy. A healthy home environment will communicate healthy habits, self-discipline, and pride. If you don't believe me, look back on the kids you knew who may have lived in the PJs (projects). The kids whose homes were dirty, overcrowded, or chaotic often became victims of physical and sexual abuse because they did not develop a proper sense of personal boundaries. Others became high school dropouts and drug and alcohol abusers. Many continued in the cycle of poverty and went on public assistance as soon as they were of legal age even if they were able-bodied.

But even in these ghettos, many of the success stories came from children who were raised in clean and orderly households (despite the decrepit conditions of the apartment buildings or the blighted neighborhoods in which they were located), where self-esteem, discipline, and love were the order of the day. What this means is that a positive and healthy home environment is not based on material possessions or wealth, but on the ability and desire of parents to take control and establish a healthy home environment that will benefit the child until he or she leaves the nest.

The next phase of early parenting involves preparing a healthy environment for the newborn to come home to after birth. As part of good early parenting, what can you do to create a healthy home environment that will enrich your newborn physically and psychologically and provide the foundation that will contribute to success in life? Ideally, you would want to create this environment before or during pregnancy, but certainly before the baby comes home. Let's take a look at what you can do to meet this smart parenting task.

On the simplest level, make sure your home is free from physical dangers and structural problems that could hurt your child. There should be guards on your apartment windows, safety latches on cabinets, and no exposed electrical wires or circuits.

Poisons and drugs (not just prescription drugs but even aspirin) should be locked up, but that's usually not practical. However, keep these items on high shelves, well out of reach, if not hidden. Guns should not be kept at home, but if you choose to violate that Dr. Jeff principle, keep them unloaded and in a locked cabinet, with ammunition kept hidden in an entirely different and hard to get place in your home.

Speaking of cats, the presence of pets often helps make happier households and can meld a family together in a subtle way. Raising pets is also educational and teaches children a sense of "otherness"—how to love and care for another creature. However, avoid animals that statistically have "bad profiles" or reputations for aggression and biting. Pit bulls immediately come to mind. Yes, if trained properly, they can be nice animals, but the risk is too great.

Make sure you have smoke detectors throughout your house. Your child (and you) are well worth the ten dollars they cost. A few seconds warning can save lives.

Here are a few other tasks you should try to accomplish before your baby comes home.

Clean and Sterilize Your Home

It is especially important that your home be kept clean, neat, and as germ free as possible, especially for the baby's first year, when its immune system may not be totally developed. There are many emotional benefits that the baby can also learn from good hygienic practices. First, it is never too early for the baby to start learning that cleanliness is next to godliness. When your child begins to learn these habits, she will also begin learning responsibility and self-discipline. Neatness and cleanliness should eventually become part of the daily routine of putting toys away after playtime, placing soiled clothes in the hamper, and other easy tasks that are within a child's age-appropriate competence. As the child continues to mature, this self-discipline will translate into such behaviors as doing homework assignments neatly and on time.

The bottom line is that imposing structure in the home by keeping things clean and orderly will directly affect your child's habits with regard to being steadfast and having pride in whatever he or she accomplishes. Remember, you are your child's greatest teacher, and if you have a lackadaisical attitude about performing tasks, so will your child.

Check for Lead Paint

In many older homes and apartments, there has been a continual problem of lead paint. Babies are extremely oral, that is, they put everything into their mouths. As the paint flakes off a wall, many children ingest it, become sick, and can eventually suffer brain damage, leading to attention deficit disorder, as well as developmental and other learning disabilities.

Have your home inspected by a licensed contractor or professional painter to determine what kind of paint you have and whether it is lead based. If it is, then you must have the paint stripped and repaint. If paint chips are peeling, whether lead or not, this condition should be corrected.

Eliminate Pests

No, don't kick your spouse to the curb. I'm saying, if you have a pest or rodent problem, get to work on eliminating it right away, since it will directly affect the health of your child. For example, mice droppings in food can cause food poisoning. Epidemiologists now believe that roaches and roach dirt can cause an allergic reaction in children, resulting in asthma. It has been theorized that the Bronx, New York, has the largest number of childhood cases of asthma in the country because of its excessive pest infestation.

Provide a Quiet Environment

Quite often when living in apartment buildings, there are noisy neighbors. You know who I'm talking about: The ones who turn up the bass on their music at 11:00 P.M. on a weekday. If you've been able to grin and bear it, now may be the time to explain as peacefully as you can that a baby will soon be in your home. Therefore, they need to cooperate and play their music on a certain schedule, specifically not after seven or eight in the evening. Why? Most pediatricians agree that during infancy a child should be put to bed no later than seven or eight in the evening. This early bedtime will assure a proper sleep cycle, which will allow for the baby's rest and optimum growth.

Eliminate Smoking and Drinking from Your Home

If there is anyone in your home who smokes or drinks, now may be the best time to establish house rules with regard to smoking outdoors and not drinking excessively in front of the baby or other children. Secondhand smoke is very bad for adults but is even more insidious to a developing child. It can cause lower body weight, stunted growth, and lowered intellectual potential. One more thing: your smoking and drinking may become imprinted in your child's mind, perhaps increasing the chances he or she will find it natural to drink or smoke later in life.

Setting the Stage for Intellectual Development

Now for some of the fun stuff! Your newborn is a sponge soaking in all sorts of information from the environment. As a matter of fact, the period from birth to age three is the optimal time for learning, since a baby's brain cells are in the process of rapid development. You should therefore try to create as stimulating an environment as possible to promote intellectual growth.

For example, eye-hand coordination can be developed by having your child watch and reach out to touch a spinning mobile over the crib. Bright colors in the baby's room or immediate surroundings will engage his attention and develop a quicker awareness of color. Educational toys, especially those that talk and play music, puzzles, and other interactive toys will develop attention and focusing skills as well as enhance problem-solving skills. What you are doing here is not only feeding the baby's intellect and curiosity but also setting a pattern of learning that the child will incorporate as a good habit and personality trait.

As part of this task, I believe it is never too early to introduce pictures, storybooks, dolls, and other tools that portray African Americans. This is the beginning of teaching pride and love for oneself, which is the foundation of strong self-esteem. Regrettably, I am a living witness of the importance of this task. In my home, we did not take the time to introduce images of African Americans to our daughter. Consequently, as she got older, every doll or storybook she chose contained only white characters. Even when we started giving her black dolls, *she would reject them as being ugly!* It is only now that she is starting to accept black figures as being beautiful. Please learn from our mistake!

There are many more things that you can do to stimulate the intellect and curiosity of your child in the home. Consult your pediatrician, talk to some teachers, and pick up parenting articles that offer creative ideas. The point is to get into the habit of stimulating your child's emotional and intellectual growth every minute you can. There will be more suggestions provided throughout this book that relate to different stages of your child's life and how smart parenting can make a real difference.

Healthy Parental Relationships

The final piece in putting together a good home environment for your child is keeping a healthy relationship with your spouse or partner. In order for your child to be emotionally healthy, he or she must also experience love, strength, and stability, as lived out by the parents. It's just common sense that happy children come from happy homes and troubled children come from troubled homes. If the parents incessantly argue and fight, the kids usually come to believe that they have played a part, and sometimes a major one, in this conflict. They feel guilty, depressed, anxious, and finally angry. Anyway you cut it, they are unhappy. Childhood and happiness should be synonymous with one another. Eventually, this unhappiness may result in retarded or delayed emotional and intellectual growth or social problems, including possibly criminal behavior.

As expectant parents, if you are out of sync and have many marital or relationship problems, for your sake and the sake of your children, you must try to resolve your issues. Part of smart parenting with your partner is to model loving behavior for your child. I'm sure you know of many unhappy couples who end up taking their anger and frustration out on their kids. The stakes are high. You *must* work out your relationship issues. Here are some strategies you can use to begin addressing your conflicts:

- Sit down somewhere quiet, on consecutive days (you won't be able to do it in one sitting), and begin discussing your fundamental differences. Write them down, if you have to, in order to clarify them.
- Offer your point of view on each issue; then listen and try to understand your partner's viewpoints.
- Discuss options and solutions that can begin to solve your long-standing issues. Don't let the same problems keep coming up.
- On some points, you may continue to see things differently. Therefore, you may have to agree to disagree on certain issues and stop fighting about them.
- Discuss the importance of your relationship and how it may affect the baby.
- Come up with rules of behavior that you will exhibit in front of the baby, especially for those times when you are angry with one another.

Therapy Can Help!

If you believe that the problems in your relationship are more than you can handle alone, try professional counseling. As a therapist, I am, of course, a believer in the power of therapy. But, man-oh-maneshevitz! Black folks have taken to therapy like vampires to garlic! How many times have I heard black people say, "I don't need no shrink. I'm not crazy!" or, "I'm not going to see some white man about my problems."

I'll tell you what—white folks have no problems going to therapy to work out *their* issues. I've attended parties where I have heard them *brag* about the cost of their therapists! The point is that they feel no shame about being in therapy.

So, listen up, black people. First of all, most "crazy" people do not see therapists on an outpatient basis; they are instead committed to psychiatric wards. Therapy is for very *sane* people who want to make positive changes in their lives. Second, there are plenty of black therapists out there, and many white therapists are being trained in "cultural sensitivity." Therefore, if you need a shrink, get one! A good therapist can help a couple communicate and provide some simple tools to help the two of you create a stronger, more understanding, and happier relationship, which translates to a happier pregnancy, a happier home, and a happier child.

So, heal your relationships. Find the love that brought you together in the first place and inspired you to create a baby. Make that loving emotion dominate your lives!

Parent, Heal Thyself

Another important relationship to work on to enhance a safe and nurturing environment for the baby is the one you have with yourself. With the prospect of a new child totally dependent on you for its every need, you may find yourself thinking a lot about your own qualities as a person and a potential parent. Think about the parts of your life that are causing you the most stress. I know it's tough to eliminate these entirely, as some may seem out of your control, but you should make an effort to change what you can and better manage what you can't.

Self-examination is a good thing. You will be ultimately responsible for raising your child, and being conscious of both your good and bad traits will allow you to enhance the best and control the worst in yourself. How will you ever be able to help your child believe in his own abilities and potential if you seriously question yours or have problems with your own self-esteem and self-worth? Have you been physically or sexually abused as a child and been in denial all these years? Well, now is the time to work it out!

There may be other chronic issues, such as a substance abuse, that you have trouble owning up to. An effective way to explore your psyche and confront your problem is through self-help groups that are usually led by survivors and attended by members with similar psychological issues. Long-established groups such as Alcoholics Anonymous and Narcotics Anonymous all have powerful and effective recovery programs and are conveniently located throughout most communities.

For whatever emotional problem you are struggling with, there is a group out there with people like you who can help you work it out. All you have to do is contact your local hospital or pick up the Yellow Pages to find a self-help group in your area. Remember, *you may be at greater risk of becoming an abusive parent* if you have these unresolved emotional issues, so work it out and get help!

The Ultimate Therapist

The most important relationship you must work on, however, to stay spiritually strong and create healthy relationships with your spouse and children, is the one you have with God. If God is not in your life and in your heart, chances are your long-standing conflicts and problems will infect and weaken the home environment. You'll find that if you strengthen your spirituality and pray for His help to keep you and your baby strong, you will be ready to be the best parent that you can. Remember, the family that prays together, stays together!

2

HOW TO TREAT A BABY

LET'S ASSUME YOU'VE GIVEN your baby good prenatal care and even a prenatal education. You've even unpacked all your emotional baggage so that you are properly emotionally available to be the best parent to your precious child that you can. Now that your child is here, what is the single most important thing you can give to create a nurturing and positive environment?

The Gift of Love

The answer, plain and simple, is love! That's all, just good-old loving. Hey, plants and flowers need love; animals need love; and even people need love. It only makes sense that babies also need love. Parental love will benefit your child in countless ways. It teaches her how to love others and to enjoy love in return. Love is a spiritual vitamin that can help a child grow strong and thrive. Parental love is the foundation of good self-esteem; if you are not loved by the most important people in your life, how can you possibly learn how to love yourself? A baby who is loved and nurtured is a healthy, happy baby. End of story!

There are countless ways a parent can express love to a child. A loving parent is one that is sensitive to both the spoken and unspoken needs of his child. When that child is hurt, the parent is there to soothe the fears and bandage both the physical and emotional wounds. As loving parents we must be the support, the backup, and even the guardian angels that can guide children through the bumps and bruises of life.

Scientists and researchers have studied and dissected the benefits of receiving parental love, from birth through adulthood. Anyway you cut it, the results are always the same: Babies who are raised rich in love usually grow up to become well-adjusted, bright, and loving individuals.

Many studies have proven that children who have not been provided parenting in a loving and caring manner, especially from birth, have trouble developing the empathy and interpersonal skills needed to make friends and establish enduring relationships. They soon begin to isolate themselves and view situations from only their perspective view not hearing the ideas of others. It's from this type of personality that people look out only for themselves and do not care about the feelings of others. This personality allows someone the capacity to violate the rights of others without remorse. Folks, I'm talking to you from personal experience. I have conducted in-depth evaluations of young black men who have committed murder and have been sent to death row. These young men shared the same personality traits of low self-esteem, insensitivity, and poor social skills. In almost every case, their parents and relatives had their own psychological issues and did not offer unconditional love, but instead abused them verbally and/or physically. As an example of a victim of this type of parenting, James Allen Gordon, age twenty-six, was sentenced to life in prison for sexual assault and the murder of three women. In addition, he was convicted of trying to kill two others. He was spared the death penalty because of his horrible childhood and upbringing. A portrait was provided of Gordon as being an abused and unwanted child. He was born to a fourteen-year-old mother who was addicted to alcohol and drugs. He grew up watching her inject heroin and was frequently beaten by her. Relatives testified that his mother often left him dirty, unkempt, and unfed. He was often forced to beg for scraps of food from neighbors and strangers.

Parents, this one is a no-brainer: If you want your children to make it, you've got to treat them in a loving way all the time, or they lose, you lose, and eventually we all lose.

All children need love, but black kids also need love for other reasons. You've probably heard of the black plays *Beauty Shop, Nobody Likes a Colored Girl...,* and *Why Good Girls Love Bad Boyzs.* A major theme of these plays is how racism and prejudice poison the thinking of its victims, in this case black people. They eventually begin to internalize all the ugly and negative images that are put out there as part of racism, resulting in low self-esteem and self-hate. The best counter to low self-esteem and self-hate is self-love, which can only develop from receiving parental love right from birth. That's why it's up to us as parents to give our black children all the love that's humanly possible and to support and guide them to total physical and emotional self-acceptance despite living in a society that can be cruel and unfair.

There are many ways and methods to provide love. The following are the most essential principles and techniques.

Positive Reinforcement

As parents, there are those occasions when we may have not had the time or patience to dispense our love in a calm and tranquil manner. When we get bent out of shape, love, care, and concern are sometimes expressed through screaming and yelling. Nobody is perfect. However, it is especially important to not yell or scream at your newborn. Initial impressions are lasting impressions. Screaming at your infant, even if only occasionally during infancy, may cause him to become fearful, lose self-confidence, and even learn much more slowly. Screaming orders instead of taking the time to figure out a peaceful and positive solution to a problem may often seem like the easiest way to handle a situation, but it isn't; it's only a short-term solution with negative long-term consequences. If you intimidate your child into submission you may win the battles but lose the war. You will have raised a child who will someday come back at you and society with the same rage and anger.

Believe it or not, the same amount of energy you put into yelling or screaming at your kids to get them to behave can be better used to calmly provide love, encouragement, and support to get the desired results. This smart parenting technique is what social scientists call positive reinforcement. In laymen's terms, it simply means getting your child to behave and achieve by rewarding even the littlest things that he does right. Steady encouragement and praise will boost your child's self-esteem and competence.

I often witness parents deriding their children (often with yelling and screaming) for all the things they think they do wrong and not congratulating them often enough for the things they do right. The kids usually end up withdrawing or just feeling plain stupid. Often they don't even bother taking on challenges because they think they are going to screw up again! This is especially dangerous for black children. One of the effects of systematic racism is that they do not receive recognition for achievement as often as their white peers. If you want your child to believe in herself despite society telling her she is not equal, you have to demonstrate that you believe in her abilities. You have to become your child's loudest cheerleader. That is why positive reinforcement must be continuous and must start at the earliest stages of your child's life.

Let's take a very specific look at how you can use the principle of positive reinforcement to encourage and increase the self-esteem and healthy behaviors of your child. Let's take, for example, a toddler who is acting very selfishly, which in the long run can become an unhealthy behavior. Some parents might simply command the child to stop being selfish and try to force her to share her toys. As most toddlers *are* selfish (it's normal) and have not yet developed the capacity to really understand the benefits of sharing, this effort will most likely result in a tantrum. Using positive reinforcement, you would not force her to do something she is not ready to do or call her names to make her feel bad about herself. Instead, make a big, happy fuss every time she shows the slightest tendency to share by giving praise (a positive reinforcement), such as "You go, girl," or even a reward, such as a cookie or a small toy. Your child will soon learn that positive behaviors lead to positive outcomes, such as praise and rewards. She will learn the lesson more slowly, but she will really learn it rather than having it forced upon her. And she will learn it in a way that makes her feel good about herself, not bad—the most important lesson of all.

Discipline—Another Form of Love

Finally, let's take a look at another form of parental love, one that is as essential as nurturing and positive reinforcement in order to mold your child into a well-behaved and success-oriented child. Discipline is that form of parental love and smart parenting that will help your black child develop the self-discipline and confidence to handle all the challenges of life. Some people call this discipline tough love. The only thing that is "tough" about this love is that it requires you, as the parent, to consistently lay down gentle but firm discipline in order to train your child to develop positive habits and behaviors. It becomes tough when you have to say no to your child. It is even tougher when you resist your child's efforts to tug at your heartstrings in order to get away with nonproductive behaviors.

Psychologists and child-rearing experts overwhelmingly agree that discipline, beginning early in your child's life, is crucial to proper and balanced development. Children raised without discipline never develop *self*-discipline. A child who lacks discipline will not do homework, pay attention in class, clean his room, or obey his parents. Children without self-discipline are often rude, having been spoiled by parents who allowed them to get away with uncivil behavior. Furthermore, black children who lack self-discipline will not develop the intestinal fortitude to overcome the inequities of life.

Though my parents have been deceased for over twenty years, the effects of their discipline have stayed with me throughout my adult life. From my earliest childhood years, they explained that as a black person I would have to work ten times harder than my white peers to be successful. This meant coming home straight from school everyday and doing homework before I could go out to play. I had to read a minimum of two books a week or I would not get treats or rewards. Hard work, efficiency, and follow-through soon became a normal part of my daily routine and life. I truly believe it was this discipline that gave me the strong work habits and confidence to tackle life and be successful. Because of this self-discipline, I have been able to run mental health clinics, appear on radio and television shows, write articles and a book, study and perform jazz, and raise a family, all at the same time. I'm not bragging here, folks; the point I am making is that I'm just an average Joe. If my parents' disciplining techniques set a positive and productive tone in my life, I know that you can achieve even more with your kids.

Discipline can take many forms, some stricter than others. Let's look at some different forms of discipline, as used in smart parenting, that can be used to mold and strengthen your young child's positive behaviors, as well as set lifelong patterns of self-discipline and success-oriented behavior.

Withholding

Withholding usually involves using negative consequences, such as taking away something that is valued by the child, in response to undesirable behavior. For example, toddlers think they rule the world from their high chairs, especially at mealtime. This is the time they play with their food or throw their bowls on the floor, or even chuck their oatmeal into your face—and then they follow it up with a nice laugh! One way you can get your toddler to stop throwing the food and actually eat is by pulling the bowl away from her for about ten seconds each time she goes into her Dwight Gooden routine. After this happens a few times, she'll begin to understand that throwing food (an undesirable behavior) results in having her meal removed (a negative consequence).

If your preschool child is extremely sloppy and will not put toys away after playtime, you can confiscate toys left out or not picked up and not return them until she demonstrates that she will clean up after each playtime.

The point here is that you are teaching your child about consequences as opposed to just punishing for the sake of punishing. In the real world, irresponsible behavior leads to undesirable consequences. If a student does not study, she will get bad grades or fail her courses. If an employee is chronically absent from work, he will get fired. Teaching your child, even from the earliest age, to understand that bad behavior brings about bad consequences is an essential, practical lesson that will be part of a successful and strong, evolving character. You are not a mean parent for teaching your child this lesson. In fact, you are doing your child a great favor.

Time-out

For young children, another effective form of smart discipline is the time-out, that is, making your child sit quietly and alone after he has been warned but continues to disobey your requests. The idea is to remove the child from the situation in which he is behaving badly to allow him to calm down and think about his behavior. It is part punishment, but, to an even greater extent, it is a way to give the child the opportunity to start over and get her behavior right. This time-out period also affords a parent the opportunity to quietly reason with the child and point out negative behavior. You should always explain calmly why you are putting your child in the time-out so the discipline will be focused and effective. Otherwise the kid will just fume and perhaps act out again. You can begin by using time-outs at about twelve months to calm down a baby who is having a tantrum. A time-out should last as long as the child needs to get a grip on himself and realize that his behavior must change in order for him to come back into the situation he was taken out of.

Spanking

To spank or not to spank, that is the six-million-dollar question. There's been a lot of discussion by child psychologists and other child-rearing experts about whether spanking is okay. The overwhelming answer is *no!* They do not consider spanking any part of smart parenting. University of New Hampshire sociologist Murray Straus has done extensive research on this topic and believes that when parents use corporal punishment on their kids to reduce negative behavior, in the long run their efforts will backfire. As a matter of fact, the children will typically act out even more, resulting in aggression, violent criminal behavior, impaired learning, depression, and, in extreme cases, suicide. He further asserts that children who are never spanked or are hardly ever spanked fare better on some intelligence tests than children who are frequently smacked. He believes this may be because parents who do not spank their children spend more time talking and reasoning with them.

The American Academy of Pediatrics also suggested that spanking is the least effective discipline method. They believe that spanking by itself does not teach good behavior and that children feel resentful, humiliated, and helpless after being spanked.

Despite this plethora of research that condemns spanking, many black parents continue to liberally use corporal punishment as a form of discipline. Why do we continue to use this outdated and often destructive form of punishment? I believe the answer lies in what we ourselves experienced as children. Many of us had an old-world upbringing, perhaps in the South, the Caribbean Islands, or even mother Africa, and that type of childhood usually included a lot of discipline and a whole lot of "whuppings." In these cultures, hitting was considered a proper way to enforce discipline. Naturally, we tend to imitate our parents' behavior and employ corporal punishment with our own children.

Hitting children teaches them it's okay to resort to violence to solve problems. Being hit a lot makes some children meek and fearful, and in others it fosters anger and a desire to strike out, usually by hurting or humiliating somebody else. These are not personality traits that you want to see in your child. Talking and reasoning things out rather than hitting takes more time and requires a lot of patience on your part, but it is well worth it. Your child learns to express his feelings in words, and to discuss, negotiate, and compromise. He learns that even when his parents disapprove of his behavior, they always listen to his point of view and never resort to causing him the physical pain and emotional humiliation that come from hitting. He learns that even when his parents are very angry they are able to control themselves and stick to talking rather than opt for violence. (It is especially important for boys—who will later grow up to be men and involved with women—to learn that just because someone is bigger and stronger than someone else, it does not give him the right to use that physical superiority against another.) Therefore, reasoning with your child and shaping his behavior with positive reinforcement, withholding, and other nonviolent methods of parenting is the most constructive way to go, with the best results over the long term.

That's the ideal, but in reality, sometimes there is that rare situation when you have reached the breaking point, throw reason to the wind, and lay a spanking on your child. For many

parents this happens when a child has become so unmanage-
able or out of control that no amount of talking, bargaining, or
reasoning will convince him to listen to you and stop his
negative behavior. It happens to every parent, even psychologists who are parents. This reckoning happened to me one
time when my four-year-old son threw a temper tantrum on a
long car trip. After trying to reason with him for over an hour,
the last thing on my mind was employing behavior modification techniques. Instead, I gave him a spanking. It was simply a
short-term solution, and I felt terrible afterwards because
nothing was really solved. Within a few days the tantrums
returned and had to be properly addressed through smart
parenting techniques like positive reinforcement and discipline.

Still, if you as a parent have reached that breaking point and
absolutely feel that you must spank your child to make a point
and address a behavior, then at least adhere to the following
commandments:

Do Not Use Anything Other Than Your Open Hand.   You must
not and cannot hit your children with belts or other objects; it's
just too dangerous. For one, they can cause serious welts to the
skin as well as other injuries. Spankings should be carried out
only with the open hand, on the buttocks or outside the upper
thigh. A brief, single smack to the butt will startle your child
enough to make him listen.

Talk About It.   Immediately after the spanking you should
have a sit-down, heart-to-heart talk with your child to resolve
the problem. Also have a mental talk with yourself as to why
you felt you had to resort to spanking and what other nonviolent
and creative parenting technique might work better so that
spankings are rare.

Parents, if you are extremely angry and out of control, do not
spank! If you are high or drunk, do not spank! Wait until you
have calmed down and/or are sober. You must be in complete
control of your emotions so you do not cross the bounds of
safety into even the slightest abuse.

Alternatives to Spanking

Let's not lose sight of our objectives. We want to use the
techniques of smart parenting to better love, nurture, and

parent our children so they can develop the proper physical and emotional abilities to become successful in all arenas of life. And if strong self-esteem is to become the foundation of their psychological profile, does spanking really contribute to this effort? I think not. The research on corporal punishment shows that spanking is not only physically but also emotionally injurious to children.

There are definitely strategies much better than spanking to address negative behaviors. However, for the strategies to be most effective, discipline must be appropriate to the child's age. Parents often become frustrated and give up on nonphysical forms of discipline because they don't choose techniques appropriate to their children's maturity level. For example, using time-out on a newborn is inappropriate. A three-year-old, on the other hand, can make the intellectual connection that bad behavior may result in having to sit in a chair alone.

The following are smart parenting techniques for disciplining infants, toddlers, and older children for you to use when you feel the urge to hit:

Infants

- When there is danger of hitting, grasp and hold on to the infant's hand instead.
- If your child is holding on to something you don't want him to have, instead of taking it away, give him another toy in exchange.
- Leave the room if you feel your temper escaping you, making sure your baby is in a safe place like a playpen or in an adult's lap.

Toddlers

- As much as possible, try to avoid confrontations with your toddler. This will only result in the two of you being angry and frustrated. Try diversionary tactics instead. Many situations can be addressed by doing something funny, such as tickling a child who is mildly upset.
- If you start to slap your child, divert your hand to your knee or a table instead. This sound will interrupt the behavior without your having to hit the child.

School Age Kids

- When you begin to feel angry with your child, clap your hands loudly. The sound should get your child's attention and possibly stop the behavior.
- If your child refuses to listen, kneel down to her level, grasp her arms firmly, look into her eyes, and talk calmly.
- If you feel that you're about to lose control or are becoming extremely angry, walk away, hit a pillow, call a friend, or go outside and walk around. Once you cool down, your urge to spank will probably have dissipated.

I hope I have provided you with enough information on disciplining your child to enable you to use different methods and strategies without having to resort to physical force. Remember, discipline does work, but sometimes you may not see the results immediately; it's often a long-term project. Try not to get frustrated if your efforts don't have immediate results. Just stick with it and remember that it's important for you to be consistent with your discipline. Rules should not change. For example, if it's not okay to jump on the bed this week, then it should be that way every week. You will have fewer battles that way. Children will try to get as much from you as possible and constantly test you. It's a battle of wills, but if waged right, then you will ultimately be successful in helping your child be the best person she can possibly be.

Childcare and Preschools

Even if your home environment is positive and nurturing, and you are providing love and discipline, the reality is that you cannot always be with your child, particularly if you are a single parent who works, or even if both parents are working. And you're not alone—three out of five young children are enrolled in day care (and millions in after-school care). You will have to rely on child care to aid in properly raising and providing loving care to your child, and you need quality care to supplement your own home program and make sure its goals and principles are followed. That's why selecting a good child care facility, and eventually a school, is a very important decision.

I have seen many black communities that are littered with all sorts of neighborhood child care facilities, some good, many substandard. You should not simply choose whatever child care provider is the most convenient. Your decision should be based on a variety of choices, and you must look around to explore your options. Talk to other mothers to see what their experiences have shown them. Then check out various facilities. Talk to child care workers to learn about their methods of teaching and disciplining kids. Check the credentials of the people who will be working with your child, and make sure the center or day school is licensed. The caregiver should be mild mannered, warm, nurturing, empathetic, supportive, ready to positively reinforce good behavior—and able to set limits.

Sit in on a play session to see if you like the particular feeling. If your instinct tells you something is not appropriate, trust those feelings and search until you find a place that feels comfortable to your own sensibilities. Consider doing volunteer work at the center or chaperoning on day care field trips to stay involved with your child's education. You'll also get a feel for the care that the center is giving your child and the people who work there.

Ask your child, if he or she is old enough, to give you feedback on how they feel about a place. Once you have enrolled your child, if something seems odd, don't hesitate to find a new situation. You are trusting people with a large part of your child's day, so it is imperative that the facility supports your own parenting goals and ideas. Beware of bullies and kids who manipulate other children—they can offset the merits of an otherwise good day care provider.

Final Thoughts on Early Parenting

There's a lot more to early parenting than just the situations that I've brought up in this chapter, but I have covered most of the major points you need to know to be an effective parent to your young child. Even more important than technique is your mind-set. Following my advice and suggestions will make your job of early parenting a lot easier, but there will still be a lot of bumps in the road. Nevertheless, I am convinced that if you give 100 percent to your parenting during the early years, which are also the formative years, your task will be a lot easier and more enjoyable in the coming years.

I've stressed the importance of giving your kids that physical, emotional, and intellectual preparation and head start. They are really going to need it once they leave home and begin school, especially since African-American children have a history of underachieving in our nation's educational system. Let's see what this is all about, and how smart parenting can help your child avoid this problem.

3

EDUCATION BEGINS AT HOME

EDUCATION SHOULD BE the most important value for black society. Because we do not traditionally come from money, our only way of making it is with a good education.

Okay, folks, with this in mind, what is the biggest problem we have with black children? You guessed it: Despite all the material advantages and educational opportunities we have struggled to provide them, they are not doing as well in school as they could be. There are many reasons for this, and I discuss them in Chapter 5, "A Mind Is a Terrible Thing to Waste."

Nevertheless, you can make sure your child establishes good learning habits right from the beginning, right from home, before school age. Prenatal education was the beginning, but real education, of course, commences after birth, and it must be constant and unrelenting. You are your child's most important teacher. Your baby's brain cells are multiplying at an incredible rate, especially during the first three months after birth, so the baby is learning rapidly. Never forget that. Babies are incredibly responsive to sight, sound, smell, and motion, and they thrive on sensory stimulation, so take advantage of this opportunity.

The only way black children will be able to compete in society, especially in light of the fact that they may be treated as second-class citizens, is by getting a head start right from the beginning, in the home, where we as parents have the most control. We've got to raise children who love to learn.

The Fear of Learning

We must, however, be cautious in our efforts to teach this love of learning. Sometimes kids can develop a fear of learning if we push them too far too fast, or expect more from them than they can deliver by a certain age. This type of pressure will usually backfire, causing more resistance and fear on their part.

A young mother was walking in the mall with her four-year-old daughter, and they were sounding out words together. When they got to a certain word, her daughter couldn't sound it out. Evidently it was beyond her grasp. Instead of helping her daughter sound out the word more directly, the mother became frustrated and on the verge of becoming angry. Her daughter started to cry, and was visibly upset about not being able to "perform" for her mother. What started out as a fun, light-hearted educational game turned into a situation where the child was made to feel stupid and humiliated, simply for not yet being old enough to sound out words by herself. You can bet that this child is not going to think that learning is fun, but rather that it is demoralizing and frustrating.

If your child shows signs of fearing a given learning activity, try to get him to talk to you about it. Fears are red flags, or warning lights, for you to help your child deal with whatever is causing the problem. You can likely come up with a way to help him alleviate the fear and find the fun in whatever the goal is. Sometimes a child may not want to read because she has some sort of difficulty, perhaps bad vision or hearing, a learning disability, or attention deficit hyperactivity disorder (ADHD), all of which are common. Or the problems might be psychologically rooted, for example, emotional problems and maturation conflicts. Pay close attention to unusual behavior and be ready to help your child work out problems. And always be ready to consult an expert for diagnosis and treatment.

Making Learning Fun

As a parent, when you bring more fun into parenting and teaching, it can make your job a lot easier and, at the same time, take away the fear of learning. If a child is having fun, fear or anxiety does not even come into the picture. Make rhymes for things you're trying to teach your child. Gently begin teaching them how to read, count, recite the alphabet, or do simple math. Be a working partner to your child's learning.

When you're trying to teach your child something, talk to her in informal, nonconfrontational situations, like during bath time or while walking in the park. Reverse roles by allowing her to ask you questions, and give right and wrong answers to see if your child can catch you in your "errors." Use plenty of positive verbal reinforcement, such as "great" or "good" or "you're so smart."

Another smart parenting technique to reduce fear and anxiety and make learning more fun is to focus on what your child can easily do. For example, together come up with words that rhyme or that all begin with the same letter. Make it a fun game, not a stressful tutoring session. Let the kid have fun, but always challenge him just a little more by taking him to the next step without expecting him to go there by himself.

A mother I know would show her three-year-old son the word *dog* whenever it appeared on a page in a book they were reading together. She let him know that whenever she said the word *dog*, it was because it was written on the page. After a while, he started pointing out the word *dog* to her. She would not have asked him to do that (unless she knew for sure that he could) because if he couldn't, he would have felt that he had failed. If you point things out to kids, they will naturally move ahead as soon as they're ready to go there, but if you push them too soon, the effort will backfire.

Avoid showing disappointment or frustration. Children will experience these emotions on an even larger scale than you do because they feel that they have let you down, as well as themselves. Ultimately, positive feelings will encourage learning and negative ones will cause children to want to avoid whatever topic brought on the bad vibes. So focus on fun and accentuate the positive, and your child will come to love learning.

Self-Esteem and Learning

In order for our kids to be enthusiastic about learning, it's not just about getting over the fear of learning, it's also essential that they believe in their ability to learn. This is done through high self-esteem, which gives kids the confidence to take on intellectual challenges and academic achievement.

Parents and Low Self-Esteem

Unfortunately, many black children develop low self-esteem and do not have the confidence to learn. This happens for a variety of reasons.

Parents who have low self-esteem and see themselves as intellectually inferior communicate those feelings to their children, who then also feel inept when it comes to learning. Too many fathers have abandoned their families or are not around their children enough to inspire them to be curious and self-confident. Even families with both a mother and father present don't necessarily instill self-esteem in their children because they are too busy fighting. Some parents are abusive either by default (they don't nurture and encourage) or by belittlement (they disparage and yell), destroying the motivation and thirst to learn and thrive.

Philipe, a three-year-old boy, was referred to me by his parents because he could not learn the alphabet and basic counting. His parents became frustrated because they felt that they exposed him to reading and learning on a regular basis. In taking the family history, I detected that the parents tended to disagree and argue a lot. The bickering and verbal abuse adversely affected Philipe and caused him to seek escape by watching television and daydreaming. These diversions short-circuited his normal learning curve.

Lack of Role Models and Self-Esteem

The problem of low self-esteem is aggravated by overexposure at an early age to highly influential media in which the successful blacks featured are usually athletes, musicians, or rappers, not scientists or teachers. When it comes to academics and learning, black kids have few black role models featured in the media on a daily basis.

Kids also develop the confidence to learn by observing proper role models—people who look like them and are successful. If these role models are smart and achieve, our kids will emulate their behavior, because that is all they know. The problem is that many of our young kids are exposed to nonintellectual models much more often than to intellectual ones, even before they begin formal education. The result is that kids may have a stronger desire to be athletic or become a rapper than to develp the desire or confidence to become a scholar or professional.

For example, some of the greatest black athletes were pushed into and through college (though many did not graduate). They had the skills to play sports (and they had plenty of sports role models), but few, if any, intellectual role models. Yet the irony is that athletes often have to be smart to study from playbooks and to strategize, so their intellect is there but rarely nurtured. They are trained to be athletes, not intellects.

Today, many of our kids' heroes are "gangsta rappers," known more for street life than intellectual life. Emulating these rappers, our kids don't show the drive or confidence to learn in school—although they do have the intelligence to memorize an incredible amount of rap lyrics with no effort! But, again, they lack the confidence to learn at higher, more challenging levels.

High Self-Esteem and Learning

Because self-esteem is essential to learning, you must address this facet of your kids' lives as early as possible. There is a major solution to the problem of both poor parenting and the lack of proper role models for our children: *Parents* must become the role models in their children's lives, and being that proper role model entails being someone who provides love and nurturing to build self-esteem and the confidence to learn.

To be a better role model at home, try to maintain a stable family life and avoid fighting with your spouse; instead, discuss issues and don't lose your temper. This will also keep you from going off on innocent bystanders, and possibly calling your child "stupid" or "dumb." Even if it is an accident, this kind of name calling is without a doubt the worst thing a parent can do. As a matter of fact, just being angry around your child will cause her to feel it is her fault, which will also destroy esteem and self-confidence. She will lose all confidence in herself because she will believe she is stupid. So, as a good role model, you should quietly work out your spousal disagreements and never denigrate your child's intelligence. People of average and even below-average intelligence with self-esteem and confidence can achieve more in life than geniuses who lack these qualities.

Believe in yourself and your own abilities. If needed, go to therapy and buy self-help and motivational books to bolster your own sense of self. If you believe in yourself, that confidence will be communicated to your child, who will, in turn, feel good about himself and feel more confident to learn.

Finally, set a good example by being involved in educational pursuits. Take night courses (or correspondence courses) in topics that you're interested in. Finish that undergraduate degree that you almost got before you quit to get married. Start on a master's degree. And, your pursuit does not have to be academic—even a carpentry or cooking course will prove rewarding. Your child will begin to see the pursuit of education and learning as an expected and normal part of life.

Anita, a therapist at my clinic, went back to school to get her master's degree in psychology not only for her own enhancement but to be a role model for her young daughters. When she was studying for her comprehensive exams, her then three-year-old daughter would also "study" by sitting next to her while coloring and drawing. Years later, the daughter loves to sit down and read or draw. It's a way of life now, and she wants to be a therapist like her mother.

Baby-sitter in a Box

Yes, education does begin at home, but many people let their children get much of their "education" from the tube—the television set. This type of education can be extremely hazardous to our black kids' health, especially because of the negative stereotypes that they internalize at early ages by watching blacks constantly portrayed as hustlers and wisecracking sidekicks.

Unfortunately, too many parents allow their young children to be hypnotized by television. Chronic television viewing encourages passivity, which is not desirable for active learning. You want your children to be participants in education, not just members of an audience. Nielsen audience rating studies show that a lot of kids watch more than two hours of television a day, yet do only one hour a day of homework or reading. The television has sadly become their friend, baby-sitter, and window to the world. Therefore you should restrict how much they watch and control what they watch. For preschool kids, the rule of thumb should be no more than one hour a day of cartoons or maybe a family-oriented sitcom that imparts good values. If they want to watch more television, instead of cartoons or sitcoms have them watch educational programming, such as *Sesame Street, Reading Rainbow, The Magic School Bus,* or *Blues Clues.* By the way, *Sesame Street* offers an excellent blend of characters and images from all races and ethnicities that are treated and portrayed as equals. My opinion is that two hours of educational television per day is okay.

You must be strong here, because kids will cajole, scream, and blackmail to get more TV time. If you establish control over what they watch early on you will be better off. This can include specials and movies that feature black heroes in order to counterbalance the lack of successful black images on television. Make this kind of viewing a family event and watch with them. (First, read up on the person or topic, and make some observations of your own before and after the movie. You'll learn more, and you're children will be impressed.) *The Lion King, The Adventures of Alan Strange,* and *Cinderella* (starring Brandy and Whitney Houston) are examples of good features.

Local libraries also offer a good stock of movies, including educational ones, e.g., biographies of Frederick Douglass and Nelson Mandela. Black Entertainment Television now offers a new premium cable station that features black movies twenty-four hours a day. However, make sure you screen some of these movies, since many have adult content.

Your children must learn at the earliest age that they have the same abilities and worth as the majority of the population (whites). Once again, given the pervasiveness and popularity of television, encouraging its *selective* use is perhaps the best way to thwart a key obstacle in the development of black self-esteem—negative stereotypes.

Shaunda, a thirteen-year-old African-American girl whom I have been working with for quite some time, is intelligent, pretty, and outgoing. She was, however, failing most of her courses. Her parents were frustrated because they could not figure out what her problem was. Finally, through much pain and tears, the truth came out. Shaunda did not believe in herself or her abilities. After much questioning, it became clear that she viewed herself as being stupid. Much of that mind-set came directly from her low self-esteem, which had been developing over the years, especially her prekindergarten years, from watching television and buying into the hype perpetuated by society that black people are less than equal. Consequently, she had problems learning because she simply thought she could not. Much of her therapy involves changing perceptions about herself and improving her self-esteem. I have also put her on a strict regimen of watching only educational television networks that offer documentaries on black history. I also have her reading books, such as The Black 100: A Ranking of the Most Influential African Americans, Past and Present, *by Columbus Sally (Citadel Press, 1998) and* The African-American Soldier, From Crispus Attucks to Colin Powell, *by Michael Lee Lanning (Citadel Press, 1998). The black heroes described in the latter book also proved to her that black people are smart and can accomplish anything. If her people can do it, she can too!*

Reading Is Fundamental

Speaking of reading, the best way to get your child on the path to a good education is to read to them as *early* and as *often* as possible. Kids have vivid imaginations, and they always enjoy hearing stories—and then later reading them. Make the purchase of a book an event. Take them to the children's book section and let them see the array of books. Thumb through several to stimulate their interest and then steer them toward the purchase of one that is a known classic. Some worthwhile titles that I recommend include *Mama Rocks, Papa Sings*, by Nancy Van Laan, *Ben's Trumpet*, by Rachel Isadora, and *Mrs. Katz and Tush*, by Patricia Polacco. Also, Bill Cosby has a good easy-reader book series for young children.

Local libraries often have group readings for children and feature guest authors. Call your library and get on the mailing list of events. Visit the library at least once a week with your child. He or she will *always* find a book that interests them. As they get older, teach them the joys of the reference section— where they will eventually do research for projects and term papers. The magazine rack is also a good resource for children of all ages.

The bottom line is that reading should be actively encouraged to ensure the future academic success of your child. Studies show that kids who read a lot have a much easier time in school than kids who do not.

Create a Stimulating Environment

Kids thrive on stimulation. Your home should be filled with toys and games to occupy their minds and bodies, and, without a doubt, a computer. Black parents should make a special effort to get a computer for the home. National statistics show that blacks are way behind whites in owning and using computers. Another recent study found that children who began "playing" with home computers at an early age often developed higher I.Q.s than those who had no access to a computer.

However, don't let them spend all their time on computer activities that are mindless, like some video games. I see kids who are at the Nintendo or Play Station for hours at a time, and they are unable to engage the world around them. I recommend games and activities that are more educational and creative. "Candyland" is fun and teaches children colors and the rudiments of board-game playing. "Trouble" teaches counting. "Monopoly, Jr." is good for math skills. "Connect/Four" helps with sequential and abstract thinking.

Encourage children to live up to their potential. Make sure their games teach them new concepts and lead to greater learning skills. Products such as science kits, puzzles, and creative toys like those that encourage building and art will bring out wonderful talents.

You can work with your child to decorate his room to reflect his interests. Letting your child use his room as a means of self-expression is a wonderful confidence builder and will develop creativity. He will want to put up his own artwork and posters representing things he likes. You can make a game out of clipping pictures from magazines of all the people, animals, cars, colors, and other things that turn him on. Make this into a collage, which can be added to regularly. This is also a good way to get to know your child better, to see what he positively or negatively responds to.

Next, expose your kids in a nonthreatening, nonpressured way to highly stimulating pursuits such as music or the arts— whatever you want to interest them in, especially if they show some hint of innate ability at an early age. Toy instruments sometimes bring out natural talents in little children. Most children will make noise out of toys (which is fine and normal), but exceptional kids will produce a more disciplined sound. If you play an instrument, let them see you having fun playing it. Teach them a simple tune, such as "Three Blind Mice" or "Chopsticks." If you want them to learn a musical instrument such as the piano, pay for a few lessons to see how they respond. Make sure the instructor is "child friendly" and upbeat—leave the humorless disciplinarians for others, or for the future if your child is a prodigy. You might even consider taking lessons in order to be a role model for your child. We have a piano, a vibraphone, a saxophone, and conga drums in my home. We each take a different instrument and play together like an orchestra—well, it's more like orchestrated noise, but it's a lot of fun.

To encourage music appreciation, leave a radio on a good station at appropriate times. Classical music may not suit everyone's taste and may seem highbrow or uppity, but there are times when the music of Bach or Chopin, for example, seems to add sanity to a chaotic world. As a jazz musician, I want my children to enjoy jazz, so I listen to WBGO Jazz 88 a lot. It features great jazz music as well as educational, multicultural, and informational programs. Make music fun and compare genres: play part of the sound track of Leonard Bernstein's *West Side Story* for your child, and then play Dave Brubeck's jazz version of the same music. The Modern Jazz Quartet has also produced excellent jazz from classical music.

Some children show early signs of being natural artists and should be encouraged accordingly. Keep plenty of art supplies handy. Once the budding artist has mastered the medium of crayons, give him a gift box of colored pencils or artist's brushes and inks and special paper.

These individual pursuits in art and music help create self-worth and confidence.

Private Tutoring

For those parents who can afford it, get your kids private tutoring in "reading, writing, and arithmetic" if you think they're not progressing as rapidly as other kids their age. Early tutoring will not only give them early learning skills, it will enable them to be prepared and confident in their prekindergarten and kindergarten years.

Head Start

For those parents who cannot afford private tutoring or may not have the resources to purchase games, musical instruments, or toys that can enrich their child's early education, the Head Start program is an excellent option. Established in 1965 and funded at over $3.5 billion by the federal government, Head Start programs are proven successes and can help your children with early intellectual, social, and emotional growth.

Head Start programs have been extremely important in minority communities because they operate on the philosophy that many black children develop low self-esteem because of their impoverished environment. This impoverished environment is often characterized by single-parent homes, familial instability, poverty, drug abuse, and a lack of intellectual stimulation, all of which will extinguish the flame of self-love and motivation to succeed. In order for black children from these types of homes to thrive and succeed in school later on, they must receive preventive and enrichment services such as educational, medical, mental health, and nutritional programs before the pre-kindergarten years. In other words, they will need a head start to be able to keep up with children from more fortunate backgrounds.

No doubt about it, regardless of whether our black children come from a single-parent home where mom is struggling to make ends meet or a two-parent home where mom and dad are both professionals and doing well financially, all our children should have an educational and emotional head start. Whether this head start is gotten at home or at a community center, whether privately funded or government funded, it is essential for later success in school and in life.

At the end of the day, if you can instill the love of learning early in your child's life and at home, it will give her confidence, self-esteem, and the edge to succeed in school and in life. She will enjoy life more and will strive to be a better person. You can give your child no greater gift.

4

PROTECTING CHILDREN FROM SEXUAL PREDATORS

A RANDOM SURVEY of 2,627 women and men conducted by the *Los Angeles Times* in 1988 found that 27 percent of the females and 16 percent of the males had been sexually abused as children. Researchers have found that while African-American children are being victimized at about the same rate as white children, they are more severely abused and with greater violence. These facts should be shocking enough to mobilize each and every one of us in the black community, with or without children, into action to address this horrible crime.

Many of our celebrities, such as Oprah Winfrey, Maya Angelou, and even Howard Stern's sidekick, Robin Quivers, have taken up the battlecry by publicly discussing their personal struggles as victims of sexual abuse by family members. They, along with countless other African Americans, have finally brought the sexual abuse of children in our communities out into the open.

There are three key reasons why sexual abuse continues unabated in African-American communities:

Lack of quality care These days many parents must work both a full- or a part-time job in order to make ends meet, which translates into less time spent directly caring for their children and trusting others to do so. Sometimes relatives or grandparents are available to help out, but most often parents end up utilizing baby-sitters and day care centers. The Children's Defense Fund reports that there are thirteen million preschoolers—including six million babies and toddlers—spending all or some of their day being cared for by someone other than their parents. However, some of these sitters and day care centers are unlicensed and of poor quality. Because of the lack of regulatory controls, these sitters and workers are not properly screened, if at all, by any licensing agencies. Therefore, the chances of our kids being exposed to molesters in child care settings increases greatly. Granted, child sexual abuse can happen in licensed establishments, and that's also a big worry for us all, but unlicensed settings are even more risky.

Another problem is the lack of proper supervision of children in some of these group settings, which allows for children with emotional problems to molest our kids.

Jelisa, a young single parent, brought in her three-year-old daughter, Jasmin, to my Rainbow Psychological Services clinic because her daughter would masturbate throughout the day. Jelisa felt a tremendous amount of guilt because she placed her daughter in an unlicensed neighborhood day care center, which was operated out of the basement of a neighbor. Deep down she felt her daughter's masturbatory behavior was related to the center. Her instincts were correct. It soon came to light that the owner's adolescent son had continually molested several children in the center, including Jasmin. After Jelisa reported this abuse, the center closed temporarily, but soon opened in another nearby neighborhood, which probably means that other working mothers will place their children in this same day care center.

Alcohol and drug abuse   It has been documented in study after study that most sexual abuse, especially by adults against children, involves some sort of alcohol or drug abuse. These chemicals lower inhibition, resulting in the emergence of inappropriate behaviors, which are manifestations of internal conflicts. In other words, really screwed-up people are not able to control themselves when they are drinking or drugging. Since alcohol and drug abuse is rampant in African-American communities, the accompanying cases of sexual abuse also occur in large numbers.

Cultural attitudes In black families in some urban areas, but primarily in rural areas and Caribbean countries, it is not unusual for one female child to be molested by several males in the same family. Although this phenomenon has never been scientifically explained, my theory is that the target child is usually physically developed beyond her years, and that piques the interest of the dysfunctional members of the family. Once one relative has molested the child, she may begin to exhibit unconscious provocative behavior that brings similar attention from other emotionally unstable family members. Now why does this happen in rural areas or the Caribbean? Again, it is likely because disenfranchised and hopeless angry men (sort of like Mister in *The Color Purple*) living in isolated areas that lack sophisticated child protective services, have no control over most aspects of their lives, but do have control over the women and girls in their homes. Therefore, they act out their frustrations against the women with little fear of legal reprisal.

On a recent trip to Haiti, I was asked to talk to twin teenage girls who had made several suicide attempts. Upon questioning them, I discovered that their father was sexually abusing them on a regular basis. In fact, these events were no secret to the village. However, no one had done anything about it because they felt Dad was a hardworking individual who deserved the respect to run his home the way he felt fit.

In the United States, one phone call would have caused the girls to be removed from the home and the father to have to answer to the authorities. Again in Haiti, and other small Caribbean nations, this type of social service system does not exist, due to the isolation and lack of protective laws of many of these communities.

What we are also finding is that many Caribbean immigrants bring this same attitude with them to the United States, as many southerners have brought the same faulty belief system with them up north. I have been referred to several cases where fathers just cannot figure out why social service agencies have the right to intervene in family abuse cases. Because of the cultural implications of this ingrained dysfunctional behavior, these parents are the toughest to reach and to treat psychologically, which continues the cycle of sexual abuse.

Predators Are Everywhere

Despite race or culture, sexual predators are all around us. They come in all sizes, shapes, and colors. They can be a stranger, neighbor, teacher, sibling, parent, or family friend. However, men abuse children with greater frequency than women, with 95 percent of sexual abuse of girls and 80 percent of sexual abuse of boys committed by men. Even though the statistics on women as being abusers are extremely low, this still happens often enough to cause concern.

Although girls are more likely to be abused, boys are also vulnerable. A new study conducted by Louis Harris and Associates found that one in eight high school boys had been physically or sexually abused. Among those who were sexually abused, about one-third reported that the abuse happened at home, and 45 percent said the abuser was a family member.

It seems nothing is sacred, as even pillars of the community, such as priests and ministers, have become notorious for being involved in sexual encounters with their parishioners, both adults and children. The point is that when it comes to the possibility of sexual abuse of our children, trust no one!

Quite recently, a very harrowed mother brought in her fifteen-year-old son, Mike, to be evaluated for depression and possibly an eating disorder. It seems that the boy, who attended an expensive Catholic boarding school, had been suffering emotionally ever since he was coerced into having an illicit affair with one of his teachers, who was a nun! Can you imagine the anguish of this mother, who thought she had placed her child in the safest possible environment.

Effects of Childhood Sexual Abuse

Even though the threat of sexual abuse is very pervasive, we as a society do not comprehend the significance of protecting our children because we are still ignorant of the long-lasting emotional damage it can bring. If, unfortunately, a child has been subjected to this terrible crime, the effects to the psyche may be even more long-ranging than the obvious physical damage. To further complicate this picture, much of the damage may not manifest itself immediately, but may surface later on in adulthood. The more common effects of sexual abuse include depression, anxiety, and self-destructive behaviors, including suicidal gestures or attempts. There have been many cases in which these children become precocious and even sexually aggressive toward other children. The long-term effects of sexual abuse also include poor self-esteem, bad marriages, drug and alcohol abuse, and, at worst, the perpetuation of the sickness by becoming a pedophile oneself.

The reason that so many disastrous things can happen to the victim of sexual abuse is quite simple. Sexuality is a normal part of human functioning and therefore an essential component of the maturation. When a child is exposed to sexual stimuli prematurely and forcefully, their normal sexual and emotional maturation becomes interrupted and distorted, resulting in a destructive domino effect on other aspects of their social and psychological functioning. As a result, they develop a damaged psyche, which leads to a myriad of psychological problems and poor coping mechanisms. For example, psychological studies have proven that even the root of many eating disorders (such as with Mike) may be the child's attempt to regain control of his body after being violated.

Victims of sexual abuse are not alone in using faulty coping mechanisms. Parents and other family members are often guilty of this too. Finding out that a child has been the victim of sexual abuse may be so painful for a family that it results in the denial of the significance of the abuse, or even that it occurred. When this happens, the child's needs are ignored, or worse, the child is blamed for it. Of course, this creates even more severe chronic psychological problems for the child.

Mollie, a mother of three girls, was referred for services after her children were removed from her home by a social service agency. It was reported that her girls were being molested every Wednesday evening at 8:00 P.M. by their stepfather. Though the girls had

*openly complained, Mollie just could not handle the thought that
her husband was having sex with her girls. She was in such denial
that she religiously went shopping every Wednesday from 8:00 P.M.
to 10:00 P.M., knowing on some unconscious level that this was the
window of opportunity for her predator husband. Eventually, after
much individual and family therapy, she divorced her husband
and did her best to make amends and care for her children.*

Warning Signs of Sexual Abuse

If there is sexual abuse taking place, you would hope that your
child would come right out and say that something bad is going
on, but more likely this will not happen. That's why it's
important to watch for signs that may signal some sexual abuse.
This is especially true with very young children who do not yet
know how to verbalize that they are being violated. To carry
this one step further, some children are too young to realize that
what is happening is wrong. It is your responsibility as a parent
to learn to recognize the behavioral symptoms of a child who is
being sexually abused.

Sexual acting out   Sexual acting out is occurring if your
child all of a sudden becomes obsessed with talking about sex
or becomes sexually provocative with other children. With some
children this may manifest itself in constant masturbation. In
some cases, little girls will become overly physically friendly
with male adults.

*Lana-Kay, one of the foster mothers who brought her children in
for family sessions, complained about one child's behavior in
particular. It seemed that Oneka, who was only five years old,
would go into her "sexy lady" persona whenever she was around
any adult males, often requesting to sit on their laps. At first it was
cute, but when she did it with every adult male who would visit
the home, Lana-Kay suspected there was a problem. Sure enough,
the foster agency records showed that caseworkers had very strong
suspicions that Oneka was being sexually abused by her biological
father. Since her father was giving her this inappropriate sexual
attention, Oneka, being too young to know right from wrong,
came to believe that flirting was an appropriate way to get
attention from males.*

Behavioral or academic problems   When a child is unable to verbalize that she has been, or continues to be, sexually abused, her emotional trauma can be manifested in both behavioral and academic problems. A child who has been for the most part well behaved may change overnight to exhibiting behavioral problems. The child may become unruly and defy adult authority. As part of this defiant behavior, the child may become either very nervous, manic, or extremely depressed, sometimes with talk of suicide.

The behavior problem will most certainly carry over into school, where you will begin to receive negative reports on your child's interactions with students and teachers. You will also begin to see a very sharp drop in grades accompanied by a lack of interest in school.

Avoidance behaviors   The sexually abused child may begin avoiding certain situations, locations, or persons. He may also refuse to participate in certain activities. This may be an attempt to escape or stay away from the person who molested him or the situation and location in which it happened. It is likely to be a very strong warning sign that something happened, especially if he becomes upset when questioned.

Keeping secrets   If you had a very open relationship or close bond with your child and all of a sudden she begins to back off and is keeping secrets, she is possibly sending a signal that something is happening and that she has some fear of being discovered. Also, the sexual predator may be forcing the child to keep secrets in order to control her behavior and keep the illicit activity from being exposed. Coercion may also be part of the abuse, in which the predator is threatening to kill the child or even the parent.

Unusual closeness to an adult   There are also situations where a child is being sexually abused and there is no overt discomfort manifested in her behavior. This can happen when the child has been convinced by the predator that what they are doing is perfectly normal. Keep your eye on any close relationships forming between your child and any adult, including neighbors, family friends, teachers, bosses, or mentors. Suffice it to say your child should not be spending any amount of time alone with any adult(s) especially in places where they are unsupervised.

Recently there have been a rash of cases in which teachers have been accused of molesting students in classrooms. In almost every case, one teacher was paired with one student, with no other students or teachers present, after school hours. These days few professionals will place themselves in a situation where they are alone in a secluded place, or without other people within earshot, to avoid perceptions of impropriety.

What to Do If It Happens to Your Child

No one knows your child better than you, so if deep down in your gut you see any of these indicators of sexual abuse, or you know for sure that something has happened, you must take the following actions immediately:

1. Sit down with your child and discuss the incident(s). Stay calm and don't blow your cool. The last thing you want to do is intimidate your child or let her think she is in trouble. Believe me, she will close up like a clam. Even if it takes hours, no matter how anxious you are to know the truth, give her breathing room.

2. Contact the police and relay all the information you have. Try to keep from becoming hysterical, as you will only impede the report taking. If the sexually abused child is a girl, request that the police officer doing the questioning is a female from a sex crimes unit. She will likely be specially trained to be sensitive to the needs of a female victim.

3. Make sure you take your child to the hospital for a complete physical examination. Also make sure that the examining physician is experienced at performing gynecological rape evaluations. The doctor will be much gentler during what will be an emotionally and physically traumatic examination for your child.

4. Your child should receive immediate rape crisis counseling. Your family should also be enrolled in psychotherapy sessions in order to discuss the traumatic event, because it does affect the whole family. If the pedophile is a member of the family, he should not be included in the family sessions immediately; he should be working on his own therapy first.

Eventually, he can be integrated into the family sessions, especially if the family unit will stay together after this tragedy.

5. If the predator turns out to be a boyfriend, husband, uncle, or any other family member, get him out of the house immediately. If the predator is a minor, either have him move in with another relative or friend (who has no minor children in the household) or place him in a private or government supported therapeutic group home. Do not allow a second chance. He will make promises that it will never happen again. Don't believe him! The predator will need treatment. Make it clear to anyone in a position of authority that with or without a jail sentence, he needs help!

   Once the situation has stabilized, the abuser can return home. However, even upon return, your child should never be left alone with the predator, even if the predator is in treatment.

6. If you suspect sexual abuse against a child who is not in your home, you should immediately contact your local child protection agency. You may feel much guilt doing this, especially if you are not sure, but a child's life and sanity may hang in the balance.

Prevention Through Education

Prevention is always the best method of protection. And that especially goes for protecting our children against sexual predators. Just as we inoculate our children against disease, we can help them be strong enough to avoid or even fend off sexual predators. The following are ten smart parenting strategies you can use to protect your child, as well as teach her how to deal with any situation in which she may be seduced, attacked, or even placed in mortal danger by a sexual predator.

1. As early as your child can understand speech, teach her about appropriate and inappropriate physical activity. Let her know that her private parts are *private* parts, and should not be touched by anyone except a doctor or a designated parent who may be washing her or giving her a bath. You don't want to scare her, but at the same time she must be

aware of the dangers of the world, especially sexual predators.

2. Be aware of your own behavior and how it might influence your child's view of sexuality. Showering with a child up to the age of two or three might be okay. However, doing this with a child who is older can be inappropriate. You just don't want your child thinking that it is normal for adults and children to be naked together, especially in intimate situations.

3. Keep your child under your wing for as long as you can, especially before the age of seven. Quite naturally, your child will sometimes ask for permission to eat dinner at a friend or neighbor's home or even do a sleepover. If you allow your child to go to a neighbor's home, make sure that you have been in that home yourself, just to have a look-see for any potentially trouble situations, such as teenage siblings of the opposite sex, family members who drink heavily, or drugs. Use your gut feeling. During sleepovers, make sure there is always a responsible adult present as part baby-sitter and part chaperone.

4. Allow no adult to live or spend time in your home who is a serious drug and/or alcohol user. Again, alcohol and drugs are at the root of the majority of sexual abuse cases; this is especially true in cases of incest. It's always the same excuse given by the father, uncle, or boyfriend who is arrested for raping a child: "I was drunk" or "I was high, I just didn't know what I was doing."

5. If your child is developing a close relationship with an adult, such as a teacher, community leader, family member, or family friend, keep an eagle eye on what's taking place between them. Get to know all the adults with whom your children are emotionally close. Be conservative and cautious. When guests stay at my home, unless they are the closest of family friends, my kids sleep in our bedroom or in my sister's space, which she inhabits alone on the top floor of the house.

6. Be aware of what your child is doing on the Internet. We've been hearing an awful lot lately about children being lured to sexual predators on the Internet. That's why, as restrictive as it may be, it may not be a bad idea to keep your kid out of chat rooms. Let him surf the commercial sites instead. You can also get public service brochures on how to supervise your

child's use of the Internet, including how to avoid predators on the Web, by writing to:

Child Safety on the Information Highway
National Center for Missing and Exploited Children
8403 Colesville Road, Suite 865
Silver Spring, Maryland 20910

7. If you are enrolling your child in day care, make sure that it is licensed and that all personnel have been fingerprinted and criminal checks have been conducted. Request a list of parents who have had their children in the center and call for references. If you use a private baby-sitter, find someone who has impeccable credentials and comes highly recommended. Ask friends to recommend someone they have used and liked; it's better not to take a chance on a complete stranger.

8. Always accompany your child to public restroom facilities. By doing so you can ensure that no offender follows your child or is waiting inside to invade your child's privacy and abuse them. Also ensure that the facility is safe and sanitary for your child to use.

9. Do role-plays using different situations in which your child might be lured or seduced by a pedophile. Pretend to be a neighbor who invites your child to enter his house to play with a puppy. First, ask your child to explain the danger of this situation. Second, ask him to come up with ways for him to say no. For example, he could politely tell the neighbor that he is not allowed to go to anyone's home without his mom or dad. If the neighbor tries to snatch him into the house, he should scream, "Help!" at the top of his lungs. Use many different situations, such as a teacher asking a student to sit close to him in an empty classroom, or even a motorist asking for directions. Throughout the role-plays, continue to encourage your child to generate different behaviors or strategies to stay safe. Remember, you want to teach your child how to think on his feet. Chances are, you are not going to be there to protect your child when he encounters a sexual predator, and he must know how to keep himself out of a harmful situation.

Life is complicated and busy. You might not have the time to use all the smart parenting techniques I have described in this chapter. But there is a smart parenting technique that you can use which only takes a few minutes a day: communication. Let your child know that she can tell you anything, anything at all, especially when it comes to situations that are embarrassing, unusual, or unpleasant. The best way to get your child to be honest with you is by keeping the lines of communication open at all times. Let your child know that you are *always* available to listen, especially in situations like these, and that you listen with *no* value judgments. When you build trust, the child will come to you!

5

A Mind Is a Terrible Thing to Waste

How many times have you seen that commercial for the United Negro College Fund? You know, the one with the young black who begins to slowly disappear, while a haunting voice warns, "A mind is a terrible thing to waste." Of course, the message behind the commercial was that if young blacks did not attend college they would not amount to anything. Back then, the major stumbling block for blacks to attend college was money.

Since that time African Americans have made major economic strides. Our middle class continues to grow. But guess what? We still have a problem with black youth and education. Though lack of money is always an obstacle to getting an advanced education, an even bigger problem is black children's attitudes toward education. Many of them have absolutely no respect for the school system or education in general. This is evidenced by record numbers of black youths who are being held back, failing classes, and dropping out of school. Too many of them turn to drugs and gangs to occupy their time and fill their lives. The slogan "A mind is a terrible thing to waste" still rings true, now more than ever.

Failing in School

Let's face it. Many of our kids have developed bad habits when it comes to education. They don't do their homework, or if they do, it is sloppy and incomplete. Furthermore, I have recently seen an epidemic of children who fail multiple classes. I remember when failing even *one* class was not acceptable. Now, it's not unusual to hear, "Give me a break, Dr. Jeff, I only failed three classes!" What makes this situation even sadder is that these kids have no idea that they are destroying their futures. Education has lost all importance to them. They really think that there are no consequences for failing grades. They don't seem to understand that failing grades in high school, even in the freshman year, will drastically reduce their chances of getting into a decent college or, for that matter, *any* college. The bottom line is that you're either college bound or you're not, and that will affect your whole life.

There are many reasons that black kids are failing in school, but one of the major ones, of course, goes back to that all-important issue of self-esteem. If you don't have confidence or belief in yourself, it's hard to learn, to study, or to successfully handle the challenges and discipline of the formal school setting. Instead, it's easier to cut up in class, misbehave, ignore assignments, and sometimes not even show up.

Another reason black kids fail is the knuckleheaded notion that if they work hard in school they are "acting white." Part of this crazy notion comes from a negative peer group for whom excellence in education is not considered important. Thus our good kids, in order to stay in favor with the bad kids, begin failing classes. The other part of this "acting white" problem is that parents or other family members sometimes inadvertently reinforce this message when they are criticizing or making fun of a black person for perhaps being a successful but "Uncle Tom" kind of guy. The black child may misinterpret that statement to mean that academic excellence (and good education) is equivalent to selling out or being a nerd.

Your job is to convey that doing well in school is not acting white but acting *right!*

A variation on this "acting white" issue is that black kids from upper-class homes tend to fall in with black kids from less accomplished families as a way of being more "genuinely black." In some ways, this is a kind of rebellion that distinguishes them from their successful parents, who sometimes are a minority within a minority. It's bad enough for an affluent black child to be segregated from fellow students who are white, but it becomes even worse when he is segregated from his black peer group during his teen years. After all, the peer group does help you define your blackness.

Raoul's parents were both engineers. Although they made an extremely good living and could afford to put Raoul in private school, they felt it was important that he attend a good public high school that offered more cultural diversity. They knew he would be one of the few black students in the private school close to their community. To their surprise and chagrin, Raoul began failing class after class. In family sessions, Raoul finally explained that he felt his parents were not in touch with their blackness and he was therefore simply trying to get in touch with his roots! To him (and to many young kids) this meant "hanging with the home boys," who were in the habit of skipping school.

What You Can Do

Though it may seem impossible to get your kids out of this negative slide, there are some smart parenting techniques to get your child back on the right academic track.

First and foremost, let your child know that his failing grades will not be tolerated and impress upon him that his future is at stake. At the same time, make it clear that you are willing to listen to whatever problem is causing the poor academic performance. If your child brings up the issue of "acting white," first examine any conflicting messages you have given and stop immediately. Reprogram your mind to hammer home the message that academic excellence is not a "white" thing, it's a "black survival" thing. Remind them of living examples of black excellence, such as Johnny Cochran, Dr. Martin Luther King Jr. and his sons and daughters, Jesse Jackson and his sons, astronaut Mae Jemison, and Professor Cornell West (who earned his Ph.D. at age 23!). Doing well in school, as these national figures did, will put your child in good company.

If your child is failing because of teen rebellion or wanting to get back to his roots, provide alternative and more productive ways for him to express his "blackness." Provide books on black history; allow him to wear more Afrocentric clothes; take him to museums; and, most importantly, set an example yourself. Keep African art or artifacts in your home (they do not have to be expensive), buy books about African-American history and share them with your child. Show them the pride and power of blackness and you will destroy the association of blackness with failure or misbehavior.

If you believe your child is failing in school due to low self-esteem, address the causes immediately. If your daughter does not believe in herself or is insecure about some aspect of her appearance, talk about it and listen as much as possible. If she needs you to be a "cheerleader" to provide encouragement, then do it. Most importantly, keep communication open. You will find out a lot about what is keeping your child from success and will be more informed on how to help.

Sylvia, a thirteen-year-old patient of mine, began skipping school as early as kindergarten due to occasional bouts of anxiety. Her mom just didn't see the harm in Sylvia staying home a day here or there. Eventually, an occasional day out of school turned into weeks and later months. Sylvia's anxiety developed into a full-blown phobia, complete with panic attacks. The thought of getting ready to go to school made her nauseous. After many heart-wrenching family therapy sessions with her and her mother, the main problem became clear.

The reason for Sylvia's truancy was a simple one—she was ashamed of her weight. We went into the problem-solving mode. In addition to counseling, we got her actively involved in an exercise program with proper nutrition. Sylvia now attends school every day. By the way, as other issues arise, she is more free to discuss them with her mom, and even other schoolmates.

Never allow your child to skip school just because he is too tired or doesn't feel like going. Giving in will make the problem worse. Your child will curiously start "getting tired" the morning of exams, tests, and even quizzes. In extreme cases, skipping school can turn into a bad habit that erodes self-discipline in other aspects of life—missing deadlines, for example, and avoiding conflicts and their resolutions. In extreme situations, cutting school can become a phobia.

If your child presently has a problem with truancy, work with your kid's school and teacher to squash this problem, and the earlier the better, because it usually gets worse unless addressed. Again, you must stay on top of this problem by being aware of absences from school or classes. Have your child bring home an attendance slip signed by the teachers every day. Finally, have a few heart-to-heart talks with your kid (it usually takes more than one!) to discuss what is keeping her away from classes or school. Then address each issue with problem-solving behaviors. Talk to other parents to see how they have dealt with these issues.

Help your child set schedules for homework and study. Self-discipline is the most effective method of maintaining confidence, success, and interest in school. Let's face it, most kids, regardless of race, have poor self-discipline and lack organization. If your child is beginning to have problems in the classroom, a disorganized personality will further contribute to academic problems. Sit down with your child and jointly work out a simple daily schedule that organizes the tasks of the day. Make sure that your child is actively involved in creating this schedule. If he follows the schedule, reward him at the end of the week with something simple, like pizza, a video, or a CD. "Incentive programs" work until self-induced enlightenment sets in!

Homework should be top priority. It is very important that it be the child's first activity upon coming home from school. Getting it done gets it out of the way, promotes efficiency in the long run, and reduces anxiety. It's the only way to approach homework.

Going out to play or hanging out should always be contingent upon the completion of school work. Don't be swayed by your child's excuses, crocodile tears, or promises that it will be done later. This is a time when you need to be rigid and consistent. You must convey that you mean business.

I am making a solemn vow. If your child learns to make homework a priority, it will be the beginning of learning to use self-discipline as a tool for success.

Praise education as being the most important value that your child must incorporate. This means constantly discussing the importance of school as the foundation for any type of success in life. As soon as your child understands speech, begin to talk about the importance of learning and school. As your child gets older, talk about the merits of college and professional schools. Be sure to present this as a goal, not an option. Try to be a role model yourself. If you went to college, talk about your education. If you didn't attend college, you can still convey the importance of it, not as an end itself but as a means to an end. If your kids see you working hard to improve yourself, they'll likely follow your example.

For sons and daughters who are athletically inclined, discussions about colleges can arise in the context of places to continue their sports participation and get a good education at the same time. They are not mutually exclusive; on the contrary, scholastics and athletics complement each other— healthy body, healthy mind! And with the cost of college being close to the average yearly income, don't underestimate the value of athletic scholarships!

As you may know, Caribbean-American households can be extremely strict. In addition, they always stress education as a requirement to becoming a successful human being. My home and upbringing was no exception. Diplomas were proudly displayed throughout the house, and from the earliest time I can remember, my parents always talked about education as being the greatest accomplishment one could ever achieve. Their words still echo in my mind today: "Jeffrey, get a good education and it will help you for the rest of your life."

What my parents did and said worked for me. I was always at the top of my class throughout my education, and I worked my derriere off to get my Ph.D. at the age of twenty-seven. This was my parents' legacy to me, and it can be a legacy for your children.

Separate and Unequal

You know what? Our kids are not necessarily screwing up all by themselves. No, ma'am! They are "helped" by a system that, despite its promises, continues to deliver a substandard education, quite often in segregated schools. Yes, segregation legally ended decades ago, but some of its practices are still felt by our children and continue to be incorporated into the structure of schools.

It's a conspicuous fact that most African Americans reside in urban areas and attend neighborhood schools, especially in the public school system. It is also a fact that suburban schools, which have a larger white population, have gotten greater funding, with few exceptions, than urban schools. Of course, this results in white schools with state-of-the-art teaching equipment, such as multimedia computers. The predominantly black schools, on the other hand, often have substandard equipment and unqualified or burned-out teachers. In addition, many of the school buildings in black areas are over-crowded and in disrepair. For example, in a 1998 suit filed by the New York Civil Liberties Union against New York state, attorneys contended that school officials had discriminated against children in predominantly minority schools by allowing them to be taught by uncertified teachers, tolerating lower academic standards, relegating them to dilapidated and unsafe schools, supplying them with outdated textbooks, and failing to provide sufficient remedial instruction. But, despite these institutional inequities, once again, smart parenting will allow you to compensate for these inequities.

Be involved in your school district. Let your voice be heard as a school volunteer or member of the PTA or local community board. Hold your politicians accountable for any educational budget cuts. Call them, write them, or even visit. Remember, they work for you!

If you know of incompetent teachers or corrupt administrators, make sure that their actions are brought to the attention of authorities. A scandal recently broke out in Staten Island, New York, in which school administrators were admitting children to a magnet school based not on merit but on political connections. Evidently, the children of public officials and friends of the school staff were being placed ahead of children who legitimately scored well on the entrance examinations. It took the courage of one parent to bring this unfair situation to light.

Believe me, this is just one of hundreds of incidents of

corruption in school systems around the country. School boards are being replaced all the time due to wrongdoing and unethical practices. I don't have to tell you that the big losers are always the students. So as Spike Lee would say, "Do the right thing," and keep corruption out of our schools.

Be a partner to your child's teachers. Let them know that you are totally invested in your child's education. Stay in frequent contact so that you know how your child is doing. Visit the school or classroom at least once a month. Teachers need to know that you care and are following up at home. Believe me, it will motivate them to work harder with your child. If you have a child in special education, take this advice extra seriously.

The bottom line is that when teachers know that parents care and are involved, they, in turn, will become more involved with your child.

Special Education

Finally, it may not be laziness, bad habits, or "acting white" that is causing your child to fail. If your child is part of the special education system, that might be a whole different problem. Special ed was created in order to address the needs of children who have emotional, intellectual, learning, or physical disabilities. The concept is humane, but the system itself is rife with problems.

Blacks represent about 16 percent of public school students but almost double that percentage in special education classes, according to a 1990 survey by the Council for Exceptional Children, a professional association of special education teachers and administrators. Special ed has become a dumping ground for African-American children. The students have often had inferior preschool training; they come from broken homes; and the regular teachers ease their own burden by "exporting" them out of their classes.

Special education programs are usually poorly funded and inadequately staffed. Many are merely baby-sitting centers for children who are unable to function in regular classrooms. For example, children with severe acting-out behaviors are mixed with children who have other types of disabilities, such as learning disorders. The classrooms are noisy and unstructured and not conducive to any real teaching. The teachers are lucky if they can just maintain order.

Children with behavior problems are pariahs in the educational system. Kids who act out (e.g., are disruptive, talk out of turn, or are unable to focus) are immediately labeled troublemakers, and rarely does anyone bother to look at the possible root causes of their behavior. It has always been my contention that there are no bad children, but there are many environmental situations that cause children to act inappropriately.

Think about it. When we as adults are dealing with emotional issues, we are short-tempered at work and at home. Kids, on the other hand, act out their conflicts at the place where they spend most of their daytime hours—school. Additional funding to these inner-city schools could provide teachers and other school personnel with more training on how to better understand, counsel, and manage students exhibiting acting-out behaviors. But without this training, the teachers are at a loss, the schools are frustrated, and our children are banished to special education.

Again, if you look at predominantly white schools, the children are usually afforded more resources to help address their behaviors and keep them in their classrooms. In these cases, special education is usually the last resort. Kids who end up here generally have been tested and judged to truly need such assistance, instead of being removed from regular classrooms just because they're too much work for an already exasperated teacher.

The key for parents of special ed students is to find out what the school's special ed resources are, its procedures, and the prognosis and options for your child.

Labels for Less, or Misdiagnosing Our Children

Acting-out behaviors are easily misdiagnosed by special education programs as antisocial personality disorders or conduct disorders (e.g., one is prone to violence and bad behavior), resulting in improper treatment and continued failure in the classroom. Quite often many behavioral problems are not related to emotional issues or instability. Instead, they may be symptoms related to dyslexia, learning disabilities, or even attention deficit hyperactivity disorder.

Here are some quick definitions of each of these disorders:

Dyslexia   A neurological disorder in which numbers and/or letters are mentally processed and perceived in an inverted manner, resulting in reading, mathematical, reasoning, communication, and memory problems.

Learning disabilities   A series of physiological (psychological and physical) disorders, related to dyslexia, which also interfere in reading, mathematics, or written expression.

Attention deficit hyperactivity disorder (ADHD)   A physiological disorder causing a persistent pattern of inattention and/or hyperactivity and impulsiveness which is usually present before the age of seven.

All three of these disorders make it nearly impossible for the child to keep up in class. Because the child cannot understand why he doesn't seem to learn, he will often feel stupid and demoralized, develop low self-esteem, and show a deficit in social skills. The result is a child who is frustrated and therefore acts out angrily in class and at home.

ADHD and Black Children

ADHD has become a special problem in the African-American community for one primary reason—overmedication. Parents have complained for years that instead of receiving psychotherapy and behavior modification, some special education departments will push medication as the quick fix. When a school system does not have the resources or patience to work with a child who has ADHD, prescribing medication is the easy option. Quite often, school administrators will not allow a child who has been disruptive to return to the classroom without being medicated. This is unfortunate, because medication can alleviate the symptoms of ADHD, but only a combination of medication, psychotherapy and in some cases proper nutrition can address its root causes.

Therefore for students placed on medication for ADHD, psychotherapy should always be part of their overall treatment. I have seen many children who have been on Ritalin (the medication of choice to treat kids with ADHD) but who have never received any psychotherapy. Many parents are just not informed enough to know the proper treatment for ADHD, and they accept the treatment recommendations of the school without question.

Parents, You've Got the Power!

Are there solutions to this dilemma? You bet there is! The key is simple: We as parents cannot trust others with the future of our children. Yes, it does take a village to raise a child, but even more important, it takes a parent (yes, one will suffice!) to be the primary caretaker, advocate, and leader in a child's life when it comes to special education.

We often feel powerless to address the issues that affect our children. We often believe that the system is too powerful to take on. I've got good news for you—you *can* challenge the educational system and win. You *can* challenge your feelings of being powerless and take control of the situation. You've got the power. Here are some other smart parenting strategies that will help you take on special education and protect the best interests of your child.

Have your child properly diagnosed if he or she is having problems learning in school. It may not be laziness that is causing your child to fail. There might be a small problem with the "wiring" in the brain. Don't hesitate to have your child tested either by the school or, if you are not comfortable with that, by an outside, reputable psychologist. Special ed rules allow for lobbying to get your own psychologist if you can prove a need, i.e., cultural sensitivity. If it turns out to be an emotional or physiological problem, make sure your child receives the proper medical and educational treatment.

Saleem was a third grader who was a bright child, but he just could not learn how to read at his age level. His parents, who are both professionals and worked hard at home with him, were totally frustrated. So was Saleem, who lost interest in reading and began to misbehave and joke around in class because of his lack of success. When his parents were told he would be placed in special ed for emotionally disturbed kids, the label scared them and they made sure that he was comprehensively tested. They found out that he had a reading disability and got him a tutor. He was not placed in a class for the emotionally disturbed, and is doing fine now.

With regard to psychological or psychiatric testing, make sure that you are an active part of the process by insisting on being interviewed extensively by the clinician. Make arrangements to have the test results reviewed by you for accuracy. And whenever possible, interview the clinician who will be examining your child. Inquire as to her cultural sensitivity and cultural competency. If she doesn't appear to know what she's doing (ask questions and judge by her responsiveness—vagueness is not a good sign) go to someone else. Second opinions are always helpful. They either confirm the diagnosis or tell you to dig deeper.

If your child is diagnosed with a problem, insist on the most effective treatments. Become involved in the treatment plan arranged by your child's school or treatment professional. There should be a three-step program of behavior modification, psychotherapy, and, if needed, medication.

I cannot stress enough that medication should only be used as a last resort. Behavioral therapies should be tried first. However, once your child is on medication, he or she should be monitored for side effects, which may include sleeplessness and poor appetite. Try to keep the dosage prescribed by the psychiatrist to the minimum effective amount. Finally, always have your child's liver functioning monitored every few weeks to see how well it is metabolizing the drug. Your doctor should tell you all of this, but some of them get distracted, so take the initiative.

One final thought: None of the smart parenting strategies given in this chapter will help your children if you do not let them know that you love and believe in their abilities to succeed in school. They won't get encouragement from society, so *you* have to provide it. As our kids are fond of saying, "Gas 'em up, gas 'em up, gas 'em up!"

6

KEEPING YOUR KIDS AWAY FROM DRUGS, ALCOHOL, AND TOBACCO

AFRICAN-AMERICAN KIDS have enough things going against them without adding more obstacles, but the scourge of America is conspicuously plaguing black communities: drugs!

According to the annual University of Michigan study on drug use among American youth, usage for the year 1997 was astonishingly high. Following are the figures for high school seniors (class of 1997), in other words, the "good" kids who didn't drop out:

Drugs	Percent Ever Used
Alcohol	81.7%
Tobacco	65.4%
Marijuana	49.6%
Inhalants	16.9%
Stimulants	16.5%
Hallucinogens	15.1%
Sedatives	8.7%
Tranquilizers	7.8%
Cocaine	8.7%
Crack	3.9%
Heroin	2.1%

Though rates of drug use have traditionally been much higher in white populations, the black community has begun to narrow the gap with increased illegal drug consumption. For example, a national survey sponsored by the U.S. Department of Health and Human Services found that in 1996–1997, lifetime marijuana use among black twelfth-graders was 41.3 percent, as compared to 48.3 percent for white twelfth-graders.

The irony of the situation is that even though the white community consumed more drugs, this use has been largely recreational. However in our black neighborhoods drug use has become a way of live—a partner to welfare, a friend to the poor, and a bad model for our children, who see drug dealers wearing nice clothes, gold jewelry, and driving expensive cars. Drugs have also offered solace to many who have suffered from the injustice and indignity of second-class citizenship. Low self-esteem is a chronic problem; it invites drug use and a false sense of well-being and then further lowers self-esteem.

Drugs (including alcohol and tobacco) haunt our communities and destroy the potentials of our children. The key to winning the battle against drugs is education; knowing the physical, social, and psychological effects of drugs and why drugs, alcohol, and tobacco continue to be abused, especially by black children. Drug use wreaks havoc on individual households and communities, and the closer prevalent drug use is to your community, the more apt it is to affect you and your loved ones. The junkie may rob, maim, or kill you or a member of your family. Pushers and junkies may tempt your kids and get them hooked on drugs while they "drop out" of life.

Today, drug use is no longer a teen-rebellion phenomenon alone. Grade school kids are learning about drugs and experimenting with them at an alarming rate. In the past, drug dealers hung out near schools; now the drug dealers are *inside* the schools, and the dealers are not just other kids—some are school security guards.

Kids are learning about drugs earlier than ever, and are being exposed right in the schools; they see drugs as a way of acting older. Also, drinking, smoking, and using drugs, especially pot, is part of rap and hip-hop lore. Many rap videos often show the characters smoking their pot and drinking their "40s" (malt liquor), all of which legitimizes drug use to our kids.

The Serious Damage Drugs Do

Addicts in recovery have a saying: Keep doing drugs and you'll end up in one of three places: a mental institution, a jail, or a morgue. Many black children seem to be heading down this path of doom. Their use of drugs and alcohol is causing them a host of social, physical, and psychological problems. Let's take a look at some of them.

Learning Problems

Kids who already have academic problems caused by bad habits, laziness, or a learning disability have difficulty keeping up in school. But the effect of drug use is even more detrimental. Drugs alter brain chemistry, making it even more difficult to concentrate on reading and comprehension. If your child already has problems with self-discipline, which is essential to academic success, it stands to reason that lethargy and other negative effects of taking drugs will only cause more unstructured and disorganized behavior. Think about it—most kids who make the honor roll aren't toting "nickel bags" in their backpacks! They're too busy keeping good grades up and meeting goals to be bothered with getting high or "junked up."

Health Problems

Because many of our children are young and resilient, occasional drinking, smoking, or drug use usually does not result in long-term or serious health problems. However, prolonged use will ravage even the healthiest young body. Let's not forget the tragic loss of college basketball great Len Bias, who died of a cocaine overdose the night before he was to sign with the NBA. Other great athletes, who normally have healthy hearts, have died mysteriously from physical exertion and unexplained causes, but one theory is that drug use can put in jeopardy an otherwise healthy cardiopulmonary system.

Hepatitis and HIV continue to be transmitted not only from sexual activity, but also from the sharing of needles. If your child is using needles in their drug use, even within their own "private set," they are slated for doom.

Risky Sex

Drug users become carefree and lose their sense of caution. Many studies confirm that drug and alcohol use by young people inevitably leads to unprotected or risky sex. As long as they're high, they're on top of the world and nothing bad can happen to them—or so they think.

Crack cocaine is notorious for increasing energy and sexual libido, and crackheads typically engage in unprotected sex right after taking the drug. Unsafe sex, of course, can result in the acquisition of or transmission of disease. I have talked to many teens who have expressed regret for having had a first sexual experience only because they were high. The consequences were bad—some teen girls have gotten pregnant on the very first sexual encounter.

My heart still breaks when I think of Sharon, a straight-A high school student who attended one of my teen therapy groups. She had gone to a party with her boyfriend, got into some drinking and cocaine, and had sex with her boyfriend for the first time. He thought he had pulled out in time (coitus interruptus), but she got pregnant. After having an abortion, she became depressed. It took quite some time for her to forgive herself and only now, with the help of the group, she is starting to rebuild her self-esteem.

Jail Time

Being involved in drugs inevitably leads to involvement with the police and court systems. Being busted for buying or selling drugs can result in a criminal record, not to mention jail time, probation, or parole. For a young black person, it is already hard to get a job because of discrimination. Do you have any idea how difficult it is to get a job when you have a criminal record? The criminal justice system makes it worse—it's tough for whites, but tougher for young blacks. According to court statistics, white youths arrested for drugs are more apt to get probation than blacks. Having a criminal record is a stigma that is carried for life.

Those Who Profit From Others' Weaknesses

Recent statistics have shown that drug, alcohol, and tobacco use among American children is high, but among black youth it is growing at an alarming rate. Much of it has to do with chronic poverty and the effects of racism on the self-esteem of black people. Other factors include peer pressure, teen rebellion, and curiosity.

But there are new, more insidious influences that have set their sights directly on African-American youth. Tobacco industry profits are hurting because of billion-dollar lawsuits being filed by the states against the tobacco industry, increasing the numbers of people giving up smoking and the national obsession with restricting smokers' rights! To regain some of the lost profits, the tobacco industry has shifted from mass media to more targeted markets such as women and black youth. Their campaign strategies are designed with these "target audiences," to use their term, in mind. They encourage, cajole, and challenge these two groups to look cool, have fun, and improve their self-esteem by picking up the odd habit of smoking. Their advertisements typically give the message that smoking is fun and sexy.

Liquor companies, too, continue to seek profits in niche markets at the cost of young, especially black, lives. There have been recent efforts by various groups, notably Mothers Against Drunk Driving (MADD), to reduce drinking among young people, especially in light of increased car accidents involving kids under the age of twenty-one, and the rash of alcohol overdoses of college students during parties and fraternity hazings. Nevertheless, alcohol consumption continues to rise among young people, and binge drinking is common on most campuses. It is well-known that malt liquors, which are more potent than regular beers, are manufactured specifically for young black consumers. Media campaigns emphasize their increased alcohol content, using such phrases as, "It is the *power!"* You got that right—the power to get drunk faster, and the power to get in trouble quicker. It is absolutely shameful that celebrities such as the late Tupac Shakur, Ice Cube, and even Billy Dee Williams have been pitchmen for this poison.

Signs of Drug Use

Let's face it, at some point almost every child is tempted to experiment with drugs. It is the rare child who does not try some drug. But these days, even casual use of drugs, especially for black children, can spell disaster. They are already at risk for so many other problems. Let's try as hard as we can to keep them out of the drug scene. If they are beginning to experiment with drugs, you must take charge and address this problem immediately!

Of course, the best way to do this is to catch the problem at its earliest point. You must learn to recognize the early signs of drug use by your children.

Physical Evidence

The most telling tip-off of drug use is actually finding drugs or drug paraphernalia in your child's room or clothing. Examples of such items are:

Eye drops
Matches or lighters
Rolling papers
Small metal or glass cylinders

The smell of alcohol, tobacco, or drugs on their breath and on their clothing will soon become evident. Chronic use eventually causes the smell of drugs to emanate from the pores of the skin. As far as the particular smell of each drug is concerned, let me make it easy for you: Anything that carries an odor out of the ordinary should be investigated—it's that simple.

Bodily Evidence

As far as physical signs of the body are concerned, here's what to look for:

• Watery, red, or bloodshot eyes
• Dilated pupils

- Poor hygiene, such as looking dirty, wearing the same clothes, or not combing hair or cleaning dreadlocks
- Nosebleeds
- Fatigue
- Lack of appetite
- Too much or too little sleep
- Manic energy—can't stop moving or talking

Behavioral Evidence

The following changes in behavior can be signs of drug use or experimentation:

- Deteriorating relationships with family and friends
- A new circle of friends
- Low grades and acting out problems in school
- Becoming depressed and withdrawn
- Acting hostile and uncooperative
- Absence from school and cutting classes
- A sudden loss of interest in hobbies, sports, or other favorite activities

Finally, if your child is an athlete and has had dramatic muscle gain or increased energy, watch out for steroid use. Also be aware of any changes in temperament, especially if your child is unable to control his or her temper. This behavior is called "roid rage," and is caused by the testosteronelike effects of the steroid use.

One warning: The above signs may not be caused by drug use at all, but may be an indication that the child is experiencing emotional problems or conflicts associated with maturational phases. Something else to consider, drug use among children, may sometimes be a self-medication for emotional or physiological problems they are experiencing. Getting them off illegal drugs and placing them on prescription medications, monitored by a physician, along with psychotherapy, is a step in the right direction.

If You Suspect Drug Abuse, Smoking, or Drinking

Parents usually don't know how to confront their children when they discover a drug problem; it shocks and confuses most parents. But there is a lot that you can do to help steer your kids back into healthy, drug-free lifestyles.

If you think your child is presently using drugs, then you need to take action right away:

- Confront your child in a very calm and objective manner, and express your concern and disappointment. Do not initiate the discussion while he is high on drugs or alcohol. He will not listen to what you are saying, and the situation may quickly get out of control. Instead, wait until he is sober. You can choose to have the discussion either one-on-one or within a family meeting. Ask what you can possibly do to help.

- Ask your child if he is using drugs. Even if he says no, tell him about the dangers of drug use, the negative effects on the body and mind—and on the family. Tell him you love and support him. Try to find out how his drug use began or escalated. Ask him if he wants to stop using drugs. Reassure him that you will get him help because help is needed and perfectly normal. (Use the cat-climbing-the-tree analogy: The cat has no trouble climbing the tree, but it's hard as hell to climb down!)

- If you are not completely sure whether the drug use is just experimental or chronic, do not hesitate to have your child evaluated by a health professional (physician or psychologist) who is experienced in diagnosing adolescents with alcohol and/or drug-related problems. Ask your family doctor or call a local medical clinic for recommendations.

- Experts have discussed the pros and cons of forcing a kid to provide urine or hair samples for drug testing. Many are afraid that the tests will put the child on the defensive and cause a communication breakdown. Black children are already at risk for many other social, emotional, and behavioral problems, so adding drug use gets them in even deeper trouble. If they are using drugs, chances are there is already a communication problem, so testing them is not going to make it that much worse. Therefore, if you need tests to get a better idea of your child's drug use (or, perhaps, lack of it), then do it. However, resort to drug tests with extreme caution. (Maybe just get a few pillow hairs tested first?) Trust me, our kids are resourceful and will learn how to confound the results of the test. At this point you will only be playing a cat-and-mouse game with your kid, where nobody wins and everyone loses.

- As far as discipline is concerned, do what you gotta do. If your child is addicted to drugs, then you are, in effect, at war. That's right, you are battling to save your child's life and soul. I don't mean beating drug use out of the child, either. Corporal punishment will not work because violence will only further enflame feelings of hurt and animosity in both camps. But feel free to impose whatever fair and humane behavioral discipline you have discussed in the past, which is the punishment for violating the rules. Be consistent and firm in your punishment. Don't be swayed by promises that drug use will stop. Let me let you in on a little secret: People on drugs lie, lie, and lie. Why? Not only do they not want you, the parent, to know what is going on, they are also in denial. The don't see themselves as addicts but more as recreational users—just hangin' with the home boys.

- If you are not making headway in getting your child away from drugs, then consider sending him to a short-term, in-patient drug abuse center. Quite often these centers are not only able to get kids off drugs, they also evaluate and address all the behavioral or emotional problems that may be the cause of the drug-taking behavior in the first place.

- Segregate your child from the drug-using peer group by steering them toward more productive peers. One way of doing this is to get your child to examine and discuss whether friends who smoke, drink, or take drugs, are really looking out for themselves—"misery loves company." Are they really friends? This will make it easier to steer your kids to after-school activities, athletics, or team sports and actively seek new friends.

Giselle was becoming more concerned about her daughter Jennifer's peer group. While driving to the market, Giselle saw many of her daughter's friends smoking pot and cigarettes, and drinking beer. Although Jennifer was not with them on that occasion, Giselle became alarmed that Jennifer might be drinking and smoking. After confronting Jennifer, who denied drug use, her mother made the decision to separate her from her peer group and friends. Of course, Jennifer refused. In therapy, we focused on the meaning of friendships and what these friendships brought to Jennifer. She revealed that having a sense of belonging and loyalty was important to her. I pointed out, and she soon realized, however, that her "friends" did not have the same loyalty. They were encouraging her not to go to school, hang out and drink, and engage in destructive behavior. Is that what true friends do? Slowly she began to realize they were dragging her down. It soon became easier for Jennifer's mom to get her involved in other activities and make new friends who really cared about her life and her future.

- Examine your own behavior, conflicts, and family dynamics to see if there are causal factors (e.g., your own smoking and drinking habits) that you can eliminate to make it easier for your child to recover.
- Kids study and emulate most of your behaviors, both consciously and unconsciously. If you don't believe me, just look at all of your parents' behaviors that you hated but started doing anyway (even wearing loud colors or two-tone shoes). If *you* smoke, if *you* drink more than casually, if *you* take drugs, the chances are greatly increased that your kids may pick up one or all of these habits. You just can't tell your child not to drink or use drugs if you're saying it with a glass of wine in your hand and a cigarette or joint in your mouth. However, a good time to mend your ways and give up these bad habits is when you start having children.
- Make a family decision about alcohol and cigarettes, especially if your teen is eighteen years or older. Discuss moderation in drinking at parties and socials, and avoidance on a daily basis. Warn your children about the real dangers of binge drinking, especially if they are going off to college.

Keeping Kids Drug Free

Let's take a look at what you can do through smart parenting if your child has not yet used drugs, but due to peer pressure is thinking about using drugs, or maybe has indulged infrequently as part of the transition from the adolescent and teen years to young adulthood.

Open Communication

As always, "An ounce of prevention is worth a pound of cure." So you know the deal! Be aware of everything that is happening in your child's life. The only way to do this, other than having an electronic bug planted on your child, is by keeping open communication at all times. Establish an open door policy in the family so that your children will get in the habit of talking to you. Then if they have any mixed feelings at all about drugs, they will talk with you first. Always be consistent, calm, and reasonable when speaking with your child. And don't preach! We parents love to preach, but for God's sake, we aren't in church all the time! If you are always preaching, you will turn your kids off. Be ready to listen. As part of the listening skills you need to develop, always give lots of praise for the things that they do right (but don't preach!). In addition, don't interrupt, even if you have the urge to suddenly start…preachin'!

Read the chapters on hip-hop and teen rebellion. They will give you more insights on why so many of our children use drugs. Try to understand your children. Know what the hip-hop culture is all about. Try to understand what issues teenagers face and why they act out the way they do. This knowledge will certainly help you interact frequently and positively with your child.

Help Them Say No

"Just say no!" Yeah, yeah, I know, that old phrase sounds trite and simplistic, but check it out, just saying no can work. However, it must first be believable to your child for it to be an effective strategy. Here's a simple role-play exercise (no acting classes needed) that you can practice with your kid that should drill the message and its importance into their naturally hard heads.

Set up a couple of imaginary yet realistic scenarios in which your child can practice saying no. Here's one example you can use.

During a school dance, you and your date are approached by

a couple of "homies" who have some "weed" and offer to share it to help you get your "groove on" and "party right." What do you do? How do you just say no?

You, as the parent, can structure their responses into four different sections:

1. Ask questions: "Why are you approaching me?" "Where did you get the joints?" "Did you buy them?" "Did you steal them?"
2. Practice ways to say no: Be firm; be committed. "No thanks." "Don't want any." "Get the funk outta ma face." "I don't think it's a good idea."
3. Offer alternatives: "Why don't you put the joints away and let's just go in with a natural high."
4. Get out of Dodge: "I think I should leave." "I think you should leave."

In the future, you and your child can pick different scenarios to practice, from news events on television or from newspapers. Try to practice at least one exercise per week, until your kids are in the clear, which may be a long time.

Educate Your Kids

Sure, your kids know the pulse of the streets. They know what the favorite street drugs are. But there are many things they don't know, such as the long-term effects of these drugs on their health. Therefore, gather as many brochures and easy reading material as possible and go through the materials with them, discussing their relevance to their lives. Just as you, as parents, need to be educated in order to fight the drug wars, your children must also be informed to be able to resist the glamour of drugs.

Know the Real Deal

Because of the enormous power of peer pressure, you should really know who your kids hang with. This means knowing their friends by name and being acquainted with their parents. An easy way to accomplish this is by inviting your kids' friends to your home for after-school snacks as often as possible. Food always gets them! Have your kids list all of their friends' names and phone numbers, and tell you where they can be reached at any time. (This may be one justification for getting them the beepers they've been asking about.)

If you have an adolescent who is attending a party, you should try to chaperone, or at least hang around for the first hour or two, or until you feel comfortable to leave, as much as your child may resist and complain.

If you discover your child has a friend with a drug problem, speak to that child's parents and express your concerns. As painful as it may be for your child, you may have to separate or break up the friendship until the drug problem is addressed. Sit down with your child and explain that she cannot be around her drug-using friend because the friend is emotionally and physically ill. But as soon as she is better, they can hang. Your child may even encourage the drug-using friend to stop taking drugs so their friendship can resume.

X-ray Vision

As I've mentioned, the alcohol and tobacco industries have targeted blacks in their media campaigns. It is therefore essential that we inform our children of this sinister sales effort. We need to convince them that the companies are selling "poison for profit," with the goal of converting black kids into the consumers of these poisons. As part of these lessons in independent thinking, work with your child to be able to look at the message behind the message of these media campaigns. When they realize that they are being manipulated and enticed into buying bad products, they will stop being influenced by these ads.

Here is a simple exercise that can help you accomplish this task. Take a walk or drive with your child through any black neighborhood. Take a look at the billboards that promote the use of alcohol and cigarettes. (There may be an equal amount of hair-relaxing product billboards: "Girl you know it's true!") Discuss how the messages glamorize the use of these products. Separate the fantasies of these messages from realities. Teach your child about tobacco corporations and how much money they earn every year, and how it's come out that they've targeted children because their adult customers keep dying on them! On another day, have them point out the billboards and what they think the messages are about, and how they have been fooled or tricked into thinking these products are good for them. This exercise will empower your kids to see beyond the surface message. They can also teach their friends how to do the same.

Partnerships for Drug-Free Children

To help fight the scourge of drugs in America, perhaps your most important partners, in addition to your children, are other parents, schools, and community groups. Here are some things that you can do with each group:

1. School cooperation: Learn what the school policies are toward drug use. Are they invested in zero tolerance? At what grade do they begin teaching drug education? Visit your child's school and become part of the policy-making decisions on what kind of drug abuse education your child will receive. Join school committees that invite outside groups to teach about drug abuse.
2. Community alliances: Know your local politicians, and assertively push for the funding of drug-free activities in your community. Work with local stores to set up safe havens for children threatened with drug activity or sales. Organize local storekeepers or shop owners to clearly ID children who attempt to purchase alcohol or tobacco products.
3. Parent support groups: Get to know the parents in your community, especially those of your children's friends. Discuss ways that you all can work together to keep the children away from drugs. Build a network in which any situation out of the ordinary can be easily communicated to other parents and addressed. Finally, sharing experiences about specific approaches to keeping your kids off drugs will be helpful to the other parents and, at the same time, give you some tips too.

Drugs are forever on the streets and will always offer mighty temptations. Therefore, look for as many resources in your community as you can find to answer your questions and help your kids either stay away from or get off drugs. Some of these resources include local clinics, community organizations, clergymen, Big Brother/Sister programs, PAL (Police Athletic League), and DARE (Drug Awareness Resistance Education). See the list of organizations at the end of this book.

Parents, keeping your kids away from drugs can be a lifelong battle, but you must never give up because the stakes are too high. Continue working hard on addressing any drug-related activities or behaviors. Your child's mind *is* a terrible thing to waste.

Here's the Dope on Drugs!

A very important part of becoming smart fighters against drugs is knowing what they look like, how they are used, and what effects they produce on the mind and body. Without this knowledge you can pack it in before you get started! Your kids will surely try to trick you into thinking nothing is going on.

Let me first recommend another great resource that provides helpful information on childhood drug abuse: A booklet titled *A Parent's Guide to Prevention*, published by the U.S. Department of Education. You can order it free of charge by calling 1-800-624-0100.

Here is the dope, so to speak, on drugs, alcohol, and tobacco.

Cannabis

Better known as "herb," "pot," "grass," "weed," "tye," "rope," "tree," "Mary Jane," "dope," and "Ganja," marijuana is the most popular of the illegal substances used by black kids. (There is even a hot new rap star named Canibus.)

Marijuana is cheap, plentiful, and easy to buy. It is usually sold in tiny plastic bags as "treys" ($3), "nickels" ($5), or "dimes" ($10). Pot is smoked either in small pipes, bongs (large water pipes), or as hand-rolled "joints" made from rolling papers. Popular packaged rolling papers are e-z wider, ZIG-ZAG, and Bugler.

Pot visually resembles dry parsley with bits of stems and seeds mixed in. Stronger forms of pot, such as hashish, resemble brown or black cakes or donuts the size of one's palm. Hashish also varies in color from clear to black and is mixed with tobacco. Pot usually gives a mellow high, which causes a sense of well-being and euphoria. It may be mellower than cigarettes, but it has more cancer-causing agents than tobacco smoke. Because the unfiltered smoke is usually inhaled and held in the lungs for as long as possible, over the long term marijuana can cause extensive damage to the lungs and pulmonary system.

Marijuana has not traditionally been considered as addictive as heroin, but, in fact, it is as addictive as regular tobacco and, worse, has mind-altering capabilities that can lead to misbehavior, such as driving accidents.

Cocaine

Also known as "coke," "snow," "blow," "nose candy," and "Lady White," cocaine, which resembles white crystalline powder, stimulates and goes straight to the central nervous system, causing feelings of excitement and euphoria. Crack cocaine, better known as "crack," comes in crystalline rock form, is extremely addictive, and its powerful effect can be felt within seconds, though it is very short-lived.

Cocaine increases the heart and respiratory rate and also causes elevated blood pressure, which can cause strokes and heart attacks. Continual use can cause insomnia, loss of appetite, and paranoia. Due to loss of appetite, malnutrition can easily occur. That's why many cocaine and crack addicts typically lose weight quickly and look emaciated.

Cocaine can be injected, but is usually snorted nasally, which eventually can cause ulcerations of the mucous membranes. That's why many addicts sniffle as if they have a cold. Crack cocaine is usually smoked in what's called a crack pipe. These pipes can be made out of anything, including aluminum cans.

A major danger of crack cocaine is a stroke. "Crackhead Bob," a frequent guest on Howard Stern's syndicated radio and television programs, is a real-life crack victim whose cocaine-caused stroke has maimed one side of his body and drastically hurt his ability to speak. He smoked crack too much, but he's lucky to be alive. He is now featured in a national antidrug television commercial created by the Ad Council. His difficulty in speaking is a sad but effective message.

Black kids are not into snorting cocaine as much as white kids, but they are the heavyweight champions of crack cocaine use. You do not want your kids doing any kind of cocaine, especially crack. It is the quickest road to oblivion. Crack addicts have short fuses and empty wallets—a dangerous combination.

Other Stimulants

There are also man-made drugs that stimulate the body and mind as much as cocaine, with all the same side effects and health hazards. These stimulants are known as amphetamines and meta-amphetamines. They go by such handles as "speed," "uppers," "pep pills," "black beauties," Dexedrine, "crank," crystalline "meth," and "speed." They come in pill and powder form, and can be swallowed, injected, or inhaled.

The black population, for the most part, stays away from these other drugs, and are not significant users. However, Ritalin and Cylert are two stimulants that are prescribed for ADHD. Since many black children have been diagnosed with ADHD and put on this medication, there is always the potential for abuse. As a matter of fact, both Ritalin and Cylert are now starting to be abused in record numbers by the white population (they're being traded for marijuana and cocaine!), and it is only a matter of time before black kids will start abusing these drugs. If you have a child with ADHD who has been prescribed either of these medications, watch out for any possible abuse or recreational use. Are the dosages depleting too fast? Is your child too hyper or anxious?

Narcotics

Heroin, codeine, morphine, and opium are examples of narcotics, which are major drugs that cause major problems. Narcotics (from the Greek word for "numbing") produce a feeling of euphoria that is often followed by nausea, vomiting, and drowsiness. Drowsiness is a symptom characterized by the classic head nodding. A tolerance to these drugs can develop quite rapidly and create strong dependence. Then, over time the addict needs more of the drug to get the same high. These drugs can be injected, smoked, inhaled, or taken orally. Heroin is a white or dark brown powder or tarlike substance. Codeine is a dark liquid that can also come in pill form. Morphine can come in white crystals or injectable liquid. Opium can be found in the form of brown chunks, or powder.

Among narcotics, the drug of choice for black kids has usually been heroin, which is also known as "smack," "horse," and "junk." In the past, the favorite way of using heroin was through injection, but in response to the threat of HIV-AIDS transmission through dirty needles, most users have switched to snorting heroin through the nasal passages.

The first use of heroin is trying to tell you something. The first time you snort heroin you get nauseous and throw up. You snort it the second time and it feels great. You snort it the third time and you're hooked.

Trying to detox from heroin is extremely difficult and painful, and most often can only be accomplished in either a hospital or an inpatient drug rehabilitation center.

Depressants

Depressants are legal drugs that require a prescription. They include barbiturates, methaqualone, and tranquilizers. Depressants are usually prescribed to relieve anxiety and promote relaxation. Their effects are very similar to the effects of alcohol. However, they have been chronically abused and in larger doses have caused altered perceptions, slurred speech, depression, and, at worst, coma or even death. Mixing depressants and alcohol, which increases the strength of both of these drugs, has caused many deaths.

Barbiturates have street names such as "downers," "red devils," "blue devils," and "yellow jackets." Methaqualone is better known by the name Quaaludes, or simply "ludes." The best-known tranquilizers are Valium and Librium. All of these drugs are manufactured in pill form.

Depressants quite often are taken to balance out stimulants, so if you suspect your child is taking either depressants or stimulants, chances are they might be taking both.

Hallucinogens

Examples of hallucinogens are PCP (phencyclidine), LSD (lysergic acid diethylamide), mescaline, and psilocybin, all of which can cause both paranoia and hallucinations.

PCP is popular in the black community, which is especially unfortunate because it produces wild behavior. Also known as "angel dust" and "lovely," PCP blocks pain receptors in the brain as well as lowers impulse control, causing many of our kids to go on PCP crazes and get completely out of control, doing damage to others and, of course, themselves. Continued use of PCP can cause convulsions, coma, and heart and lung failure. PCP comes in powder, liquid, and pill form, and therefore can be taken orally, injected, or sprayed on marijuana joints or cigarettes.

LSD also carries the name "acid," "dots," and "purple haze." It can be taken in tablet form or licked off small pieces of paper. The dots are tiny, but don't be fooled; they are extremely powerful. Mescaline, also known as "mesc," comes in tablet form and can usually be chewed or smoked. Psilocybin, a type of mushroom, is eaten and is sometimes cooked in food. It produces a more powerful high than marijuana and gives a sense of well-being, but it can cause hallucinations.

"Designer" Drugs

Black-market chemists have modified the molecular structure of some legal drugs to produce so-called designer drugs. Sometimes these drugs are much stronger than the ones they originally copied, but the dosage strength is not visually apparent. That's why there are so many accidental overdoses among young people; they just don't know how lethal these drugs really are. They are so strong that sometimes as little as one dose can cause long-term anxiety, depression, impaired perception, and even brain damage.

The most popular designer drugs are synthetic heroin, "China White," and "ecstasy" (or MDMA, short for methylenedioxymethamphetamine). All of these drugs provide an initial euphoria and sense of well-being. However, continued use can cause tremors, impaired speech, and paralysis. All of them usually come in white powder form and are either snorted, inhaled, or injected. These drugs are too powerful to cause an addiction but are used on special occasions (parties and proms), and give a euphoric jolt. A recent study indicates that ecstasy can cause long-term genetic damage and has caused brain damage in animals.

Rohypnol ("Roofies")

Rohypnol is the brand name of a drug called flunitrazepam, on the street better known as "roofies." It is a sedative that is ten times more powerful than Valium and has gained a notorious reputation as the "date rape drug." With no taste or odor, it can be slipped into an alcoholic drink and cause dizziness and disorientation, ultimately causing the victim to pass out for hours without remembering what transpired.

Anabolic Steroids

Steroids were artificially created in the laboratory back in the 1930s to mimic the effects of the male sex hormone testosterone, and have been used legitimately to treat severe burns and certain types of breast cancer. Steroid use has also become a popular illegal drug for athletes. The abuse of steroids has literally been on trial in Germany—six sports officials from the former East Germany have been accused of routinely giving nineteen of their female Olympic swimmers banned steroids between 1975 and 1989 to make them stronger and faster. Weightlifters and wrestlers are attracted to steroids to quickly increase their muscle mass and definition without the traditional method of extensive workouts.

The major problem with steroid use is the aftereffects. In men, this can cause impotence, sterility, and withered testicles. In women, steroids create masculine traits such as breast reduction and facial hair. Prolonged use of steroids can cause heart attacks, strokes, depression, and sterility. Secondary side effects of steroid use include purple or red spots on the body, swelling of the feet and lower legs, darkening of the skin, and unpleasant breath odor, as well as the inability to control one's temper.

Kevin was referred by his school for aggressive behavior (in the past against fellow students), which culminated in his physically threatening a teacher. He was a gentle giant, an imposing 220-pound, six-foot, two-inch-tall wrestler who also lifted weights. His aggressive behavior, which had arisen in the past month, was puzzling because he had no previous record of violence or aggressive behavior. In therapy, Kevin was perplexed by his own

*behavior, admitting, "I don't know why I'm so angry all the time."
After a few sessions Kevin casually stated that he was getting
stronger because he was on a "vitamin program." In fact, he was
on steroids but thought they were the same as vitamins. After I
told him about the dangers of steroids and roid rage, he had to see
a physician for help in getting off the drugs.*

African-American children have not indulged in steroid use to
any alarming degree. However, with many black children
involved in athletics, especially team sports, they may be
tempted to use steroids as a shortcut to enhance physical
development and ability. If your child is into sports, stay
vigilant to the warning signs of steroid use but, more importantly, warn them beforehand—boys don't want to grow breasts
and girls don't want to grow beards—that's a simple sales
pitch.

Inhalants

Inhalants include nitrous oxide, amyl nitrate, butyl nitrate,
chlorohydrocarbons, and hydrocarbons. Deeply inhaling the
vapors of these drugs can cause a quick and joyful high that
only lasts a few minutes. However, even short-term use of these
drugs can cause nausea, sneezing, coughing, nosebleeds, headaches, as well as involuntary urination and defecation. Long-
term sniffing or inhaling can cause permanent damage to the
nervous system.

Nitrous oxide, better known as laughing gas, is sold in small
eight-gram metal cylinders with a balloon or pipe propellant.
Amyl nitrate, also known as "poppers" or "snappers" (you snap
them in half and inhale, especially during sex, before orgasm),
is a clear yellowish liquid in ampules. Butyl nitrate, better
known as "rush," "bullet," and "climax" comes in small bottle
cylinders. Chlorohydrocarbons are represented by aerosol
sprays or cleaning fluids, and can be found in spraypaint cans.
The hydrocarbons are actually solvents and can also be found in
gasoline, glue, and paint thinner.

Folks, our black kids are starting to use inhalants in record
numbers. Why? These drugs are cheap, plentiful, easy to
purchase, and can easily be found in bathroom and kitchen
cabinets. Very young children as young as age five and up are

starting to sniff airplane glue and the white creamy glues. So you need to be very careful about keeping solvents and other chemicals in the home.

Alcohol and Tobacco

Alcohol and tobacco are legal drugs that can be as dangerous as any illegal substance if abused. In some ways, they can be more dangerous because they are more socially acceptable, abundant, and their abuse can be disguised.

Alcohol

Alcohol use over prolonged periods can cause permanent damage to vital organs such as the brain and liver. Pregnant mothers who drink are more apt to give birth to low-weight babies and, in worse cases, can give birth to babies with fetal alcohol syndrome. Alcohol in young people impairs judgment and lowers inhibitions, both of which can lead to self-destructive behaviors such as violence and physical abuse, and to unwanted pregnancies.

Black kids seem to have their own culture on drinking. The most popular type of alcohol among adolescents and teens is beer, particularly malt liquor. Beer is bad enough, but malt liquor is worse, having several times the percentage of alcohol compared to regular beer. Malt liquors have become the companion drug to marijuana. In fact, the "home boys" (in the baggy pants) have created a new scene which involves smoking pot and drinking malt liquor together. They get "faced," as they like to call it, or smashed. Schlitz Malt Liquor Bull, Old English 800, St. Ides, and Colt 45 are the popular brand names to watch out for.

Tobacco

Tobacco is responsible for the deaths of over one hundred thousand people each year. It is the chief cause of coronary heart disease and lung cancer, and also can cause cancer of the larynx, esophagus, bladder, pancreas, and kidneys. Smoking cigarettes during pregnancy is risky because smoking mothers are more apt to have spontaneous abortions or preterm births and to produce low-birth-weight babies

Though the use of chewing tobacco and snuff (powdered tobacco) is rare in the black community, you still need to be on the alert for it. It is commonly sold in cellophane pouches, with a very popular brand being Red Man. The kids usually take a pinch and stuff it between the cheek and gum. Because of the accumulation of the gastric juices, saliva, and tobacco fluids, users must spit often. Many of our kids (and parents) have been fooled into thinking that chewing tobacco is harmless because it is not inhaled. This is the furthest thing from the truth and another fact that the tobacco companies hide from the public. The risk of cancer from chewing tobacco is just as high as from smoking it. As a matter of fact, cancers of the mouth and other associated areas have continued to rise.

Smoking, in truth, causes bad breath, fuzzy thinking, impotence, lung cancer, and ultimately death. Tell your children that if they want bad breath, bad grades, sex problems, and a slow death they ought to consider smoking. Sometimes the "negative sales" approach works to discourage bad behavior, so you should try it! Also, ask the school principal to show the video in which a pathologist cuts open the lungs of a dead smoker and compares the tar-ridden organ to that of a nonsmoker.

Herbal Tobacco Substitutes

Trendy herbal substitutes for cigarettes and snuff are now being sold in smoke shops, convenience stores, and, would you believe, in health food stores. These substitutes are made from blends of herbs, honey soaked tea leaves, process-flavored lettuce, and flower petals. The more popular brands of herbal cigarettes are Herbal Gold and Honey Rose. The herbal snuffs are Dipstop and Bacc-Off, to name a few. Though it is true that these products are nicotine free, they still have varying amounts of tar. Kids erroneously think that they cannot get diseases using these tobacco substitutes, but studies show that health risks still exist from smoking any kind of cigarette. Inhaling smoke, with or without nicotine, is bad for the human body.

Don't be fooled, parents—herbal tobacco is not good for your children. As one health official put it, "You're supposed to eat your vegetables, not smoke them."

General Reading List for Parents
(approved by the Partnership for a Drug-Free America www.drugfreeamerica.org)

Buzzed: The Straight Facts About the Most Used and Abused Drugs, From Alcohol to Ecstasy, by Cynthia Kuhn, Ph.D., et al., 1998. W. W. Norton and Company. $14.95.

The Fact Is...Hispanic Parents Can Help Their Children Avoid Alcohol and Other Drug Problems. 1989. National Clearinghouse for Alcohol and Drug Information, P.O. Box 2345, Rockville, MD 20852. Free.

The Fact Is...You Can Prevent Alcohol and Other Drug Problems Among Elementary School Children. 1988. National Clearinghouse for Alcohol and Drug Information, P.O. Box 2345, Rockville, MD 20852. Free.

The Fact Is...You Can Prevent Alcohol and Other Drug Use Among Secondary School Students. 1989. National Clearinghouse for Alcohol and Drug Information, P.O. Box 2345, Rockville, MD 20852. Free.

A Parent's Guide to Prevention: Growing Up Drug Free. U.S. Department of Education, National Clearinghouse for Alcohol and Drug Information, P.O. Box 2345, Rockville, MD 20852; telephone (800) 624-0100.

Preparing for the Drug-Free Years: A Family Activity Book, by J. David Hawkins, et al., 1988. Developmental Research and Programs, Box 85746, Seattle, WA 98145. $10.95.

Team Up for Drug Prevention With America's Young Athletes. Drug Enforcement Administration, Demand Reduction Section, 1405 I St., NW, Washington, DC 20537. Free.

Ten Steps to Help Your Child Say "No": A Parent's Guide. 1986. National Clearinghouse for Alcohol and Drug Information, P.O. Box 2345, Rockville, MD 20852. Free.

What Every Parent Can Do About Teenage Alcohol and Drug Abuse: Hope and Help From Parents Who Have Been There. Parents and Adolescents Recovering Together Successfully (PARTS), 12815 Stebick Court, San Diego, CA 92130; telephone (800) 420-7278. $9.95 (money back guarantee).

What Works: Schools Without Drugs. 1986, revised in 1989. U.S. Department of Education, National Clearinghouse for Alcohol and Drug Information, P.O. Box 2345, Rockville, MD 20852. Free.

Young Children and Drugs: What Parents Can Do. 1987. the Wisconsin Clearing House, 1954 E. Washington Ave., Madison, WE 53704. $6.00 for 100 brochures.

7

LET'S TALK ABOUT SEX, BABY!

WHEN THE VIDEO by Salt and Peppa called *Let's Talk About Sex* came out, it revealed that a lot of young people were having sex—a *lot* of sex. Indeed, the numbers are high. According to the Commission on Adolescent Sexual Health, three quarters of boys and half of the girls aged fifteen to nineteen have engaged in sexual intercourse. The numbers are probably greater for sex play or heavy petting.

As you would expect, the big numbers have brought big problems, proving that our kids have not only been irresponsible but reckless with their health and their futures. Many are getting into trouble through unexpected and unwanted pregnancies, while others are coming down with venereal diseases in record numbers. Syphilis and gonorrhea, which were once diseases of the past, are impacting black children especially hard. Even though syphilis is at its lowest level since 1941, the Centers for Disease Control and Prevention (CDC) have found that rates of this disease are rising disproportionately among blacks, with 22 cases per 100,000 in 1997, versus 0.5 cases per 100,000 for whites.

HIV-AIDS has also reached epidemic proportions among black teens. According to the CDC, blacks aged thirteen to twenty-four account for 63 percent of all new HIV infections, even though African Americans only make up 13 percent of the

U.S. population. These tragic statistics are due in part to our kids feeling invulnerable to HIV-AIDS: "It won't happen to me." According to Yale University's Center for Interdisciplinary Research on AIDS, despite HIV educational initiatives targeted at children of all ages, nearly nine out of ten youth still remain in denial and do not think they can easily get HIV through heterosexual sex. But they do. So now more than ever we must help our children to come to grips with and mature through the various stages of sexuality in a healthy way.

A Lack of Parental Leadership

Children making choices about sex without proper parental guidance is as dangerous as playing Russian roulette with a six shooter that has *five* bullets! The odds of a positive outcome are not good. Regardless, this lack of parental involvement continues to deteriorate. According to a 1998 Time/CNN telephone poll, 45 percent of American teenagers are learning about sex from friends. Twenty-nine percent are getting the info from television, and fewer than 8 percent are being educated from parents and schools. As Gomer Pyle would have said, "Shame, shame, shame!" Parents, you know it and I know it: Our kids should be learning about sex from us, the leaders of the pack— even if we don't know what we're doing! We should not be abdicating our responsibility and allowing such an important part of our kid's education to be gotten on the streets. Having sex is serious business, and if our children do not know the score it can screw up the rest of their lives.

Silence Equals Disaster

There are many political factions in America who hold on to the outdated notion that the best way to keep our kids from becoming sexually active is by keeping them in the dark about sex and sexuality. Now *that's* ignant! (Ebonics for ignorant.)

Many organized religions preach against premarital sex and hold that no one should use contraception. Now, I'm an old-fashioned Catholic and do not feel comfortable criticizing the church, but at the same time, with what's happening in our society—teen pregnancies and sexually transmitted diseases on the rise in black communities—this head-in-the-sand approach just does not work. Let's get a grip. Children are dying, babies are being born to babies, and, worse still, these problems continue unabated. Teen pregnancy rates are much higher in the United States than in many other developed countries—twice as high as in England and Canada, and nine times as high as in the Netherlands or Japan. The African-American community is especially affected by this problem. The birth rate for African-American teens is 108 per thousand females aged fifteen to nineteen, compared to 40 births per thousand for white females aged fifteen to nineteen. To illuminate this fact, just take a drive through some of the minority neighborhoods in your town and you will see young adolescent and teenage girls pushing strollers down the street. On top of that, millions of black babies are being born into homes where the parents are too young to carry out their responsibilities, leaving grandmothers or other relatives, or even foster care having to raise these children. Only in the black community do I see so many grandmothers spending their retirement years raising their kid's kids.

Sade, one of the girls in the adolescent group at one of my Rainbow clinics, is a prime example of this type of scenario. She is only thirteen, but has a one-year-old daughter. Her grandmother has become the legal custodian of the baby. And here's the irony of the whole thing: She became pregnant with the baby after having sex her first and only time. When asked in group therapy how this could have happened to her, she replied that she saw nothing wrong with her situation, that, in fact, she had several girlfriends who were pregnant before the age of fifteen and their kids were being raised by relatives or placed into foster care!

If Sade and her friends are so cavalier about their experiences, the future does not look rosy with regard to black children, their sexuality, and its consequences. This is yet another warning that we must pull our heads up out of the sand, especially in the African-American community. We must look this problem straight in the eye and handle it, for the sake of our children.

What You Don't Know Can Kill You!

In my opinion, the high rates of sexually transmitted diseases, as well as teen pregnancies, are directly due to a lack of sexual education. You know it and I know it: Sex is not just about "gettin it on" or "knockin boots." It's much more complicated than that. Sexual ignorance results in some very unhealthy practices and behaviors. Many of my young patients are presently facing the following issues and predicaments:

Unprotected sex is still rampant. Again, many kids just don't think they can get HIV from heterosexual sex. They think it can only happen to drug abusers and gays.

Kids use condoms improperly. The availability and social acceptance of condoms has in many ways promoted safer sex. But when kids do use condoms, too often they use them improperly. For example, they use petroleum jelly as a lubricant. The problem is that this substance actually eats through the rubber. They should instead be using water-based jellies, such as K-Y brand.

Kids use the wrong condoms. Not all condoms are created equal. Some offer better protection from venereal disease than others. There are still kids as well as adults out there who use lambskin condoms. It's true they offer greater sensitivity, but they are also more porous, allowing for the transmission of venereal disease. Unmarried people should use only condoms made from latex. Also, many kids are surprised when their condoms break during sexual encounters. What they don't realize is that the condoms break because of too much friction. They need to be told that sex with condoms should not be rough sex. Hell, a lot of adults don't even know that!

Kids are having risky kinds of sex. Known as deep impact, anal sex has become a popular method of birth control among black adolescent boys and girls. The kids are right in thinking you can't get pregnant this way, but guess what—the probability of catching HIV or AIDS increases tremendously. This is due to the simple fact that the anus has less elasticity than the vagina and is much more likely to tear and bleed. The blood-to-sperm connection is the best conduit for the transmission of HIV.

Kids are making sport out of having multiple partners. Some kids are having "hooky parties," where they skip school and have group sex in a home that is unattended by a parent. Drinking wine and beer and smoking pot is an essential part of these parties. The use of these chemicals usually results in impaired judgment and less caution in safer sex practices.

Intentionally getting pregnant. There are many young girls who have never felt loved by their parents, and therefore believe that if they have a baby they'll finally have someone they can love and who can love them unconditionally. Sadly, many of our young girls are intentionally having sex in order to have these babies, even if it means they are totally unprepared emotionally, educationally, and financially. Subsequently, hidden pregnancies, where the family, especially parents, don't learn about the pregnancies until the final months are common. As part of this scenario, these "babies having babies" do not seek prenatal care, even if it is available. At birth, both the young moms and babies end up being at risk of illness and complications.

Jazzy, one of my teenage female clients, was brought to Rainbow by exasperated parents. She was five months pregnant when her parents finally discovered it. As is typical, she had gotten pregnant intentionally because she felt ignored and unloved by her parents, who of course really did love her. After much crying, screaming, and yelling by Jazzy and her parents, her mother immediately took charge and got her the prenatal care that she had missed. Though it has been difficult, both Jazzy and her mother are raising the baby. Most stories do not have this relatively happy ending.

Push, Push, in the Bush!

It's not just ignorance that is at the root of the problem of youth sex. There is also the fact that a lot of the feelings of invulnerability, and therefore increasing promiscuity, come not only from curiosity and rebellion but also the media. Think about it: Today's advertisements promote sex and fun as being one entity. Magazine advertisements typically show young people in various stages of nudity. Remember the Calvin Klein advertisements that showed pubescent boys and girls in their underwear? But even in movies and television, sexual images and sexuality abound, convincing young children that it's okay to have a boyfriend or girlfriend before they even finish kindergarten!

You've probably seen some of the rap or hip-hop videos your kids typically check out. Admit it, those videos are so sexually explicit, they even turn *you* on! The rapper Luke from Two Live Crew has so many chicks gyrating their backsides that I can't decide whether to keep watching or take Dramamine. What about the lyrics to some of the hip-hop, R&B songs along the lines of "I want to sex you up," "give me that thang," and "I want to do it to ya till you scream!" If these words and images don't get your kids sexually charged up, then chickens *do* have lips.

Another reason for our children's early sexuality is simply biology. Many scientists theorize that our kids are physically maturing much faster than we did. Let's face it, kids are physically maturing earlier than ever before. Girls are getting their periods at ages eleven and twelve. Boys are entering puberty at similar ages. They are also growing taller and faster than we ever did. It's now hard to tell the difference between some twelve-year-olds and some twenty-year-olds. Scientists believe that this change in growth pattern is related to the hormones in the foods we eat. And if there's one thing our kids love to do, it is eat!

The fact remains that our kids are sexually active and at a much earlier age. And the kids who are not already active are pressured to start. Perhaps the strongest pressure comes from friends or peers. As with any other behavior, not just sexual, kids cave in to peer pressure because they believe that if they don't "do it," they will not be accepted by their friends, or may be even rejected by a boyfriend or girlfriend—and sometimes they are.

Sex Education Is a Must!

Sex is a natural part of life. As children grow, sexuality becomes a maturational, developmental, and psychological border that must be met and crossed. If we want them to journey safely, we must teach them to be responsible. We must teach them about sex. The late Dr. Mary S. Calderone, who was a physician and a pioneer advocate of sexual education and the cofounder of the Sex Information and Educational Council of the United States, spent her life convincing America that children needed to be taught about sex. Ignorance about it would force the child and the family to face tragic consequences.

A major barrier in speaking to our kids and teens about sex is our own feeling of being uncomfortable. This may come from the fact that many of our parents treated sex as a taboo subject that needed no discussion. We must break this generational dysfunction and be forthcoming with our teens about sexuality in order for them to see sex as an essential part of life that must be treated with careful thought and the highest regard. Teaching and discussing sex with our children is the best way to help them recognize their own sexuality in a normal, healthy, and responsible manner.

Recently a young black father came into Rainbow so that he and his thirteen-year-old son could discuss the impact of his decision to take full custody of this boy. The father stated that he had had sex only once with the boy's mother (whom he never loved), and she became pregnant with him. He felt that his ignorance and attitude about sex (he saw it as a conquest) led to the calamitous consequence of pregnancy. However, his son suffered the most because he became an emotional Ping-Pong ball between them. He further stated that one of the reasons he sought and won custody of his child was because the mother refused to talk with the boy about sexuality, beyond explaining it was a "dirty thing." He did not want his son to be as ignorant about sex as he was as a teenager, and instead chose to guide him through the development of a healthier sense of self and sexuality.

Okay, so I have managed to convince you, if you weren't convinced already, that we must educate our children about sex. Talking to your kids about sex, however, can be real tough. One reason may be that there are already some existing communication problems, and therefore talking about something as personal or even as embarrassing as sex is a whole lot tougher. Second, we parents may be inhibited and have somewhat antiquated views of sexuality. There are many more reasons, but this is the time when we are forced to bite the bullet and do the deed of sex education. Following are some suggestions to help you in talking with your child on everything they want to know about sex and *shouldn't* be afraid to ask!

Structure your talks around your teens' concerns. As I stated earlier in the chapter, when it comes to talking with teens about sex, sometimes it's hard to know where to begin. However, there is a specific smart parenting strategy that you can use in speaking with your teen on this topic. I call it the listen-and-respond technique. Basically, this is how it works: You strike up any normal or neutral conversation with your teen and actively *listen* for any questions, concerns, or references about sex or sexuality. Next, you simply *respond* to the question or the concern with your own question or statement, which will draw out our teen's concern. This is an excellent way to directly address those areas of sexuality that your teen needs to talk about. Here's an example of listen-and-respond that I taught to a parent, which she utilized in a family session:

Teen: I saw an article in the paper today about a doctor who performed abortions being killed by a sniper. Protesters said he was killing unborn babies.

Mom: What do you think about abortion? Is it right or wrong?

Teen: I think if a girl were to get pregnant she should have the right to choose what to do.

Mom: If that girl got pregnant and was underage, do you think she should consult with her mom and dad?

Teen: I definitely think she should speak to her mom.

Mom: What do you think her mom can do to make it more comfortable for her to speak about the pregnancy?

Teen: I think her mom should let her know that it's okay to talk about anything, especially getting pregnant.

Mom: What sorts of things do you think I could tell you that might keep you from getting into that same situation?

Again, as you can see, mom was able to engage in a conversation about sex with her daughter by simply listening to her questions and concerns about a neutral event and then responding with her own questions and comments. She was finally able to turn the conversation into a more personal situation. You should practice the listen-and-respond technique with your teen every single day in order to perfect this skill; it really works.

Always keep in mind that sexuality is part of life. Parents often treat developing adolescent and teen sexuality as a stage that is inconvenient and foreboding. This negative attitude can easily influence the type of communication, or noncommunication, established between a parent and teenager. It can also cause our children to develop a very unhealthy attitude about sexuality, which is also as dangerous as being uninformed about sex. Therefore, it is extremely important that we, as parents, always keep in mind that our children's developing sexuality is a healthy and natural part of their lives with which the family must come to terms. Parents should also keep in mind that sexuality is much more than just "doing it." Sexuality is the basic foundation of health and happiness. To repress its expression or view it as something unnatural will inevitably lead to long-term emotional conflicts which will affect future interpersonal relationships, such as friendships and marriage. Therefore, educating and speaking to our children about sex should become a family tradition and responsibility—one that should be approached with enthusiasm and not dread.

Get educated about sex. A lot of things our kids are dealing with today, especially HIV, were not part of our generational concerns. Learn about all sexually transmitted diseases, including herpes and viral warts. Also learn about the best protection that is available. Read parenting and youth-oriented magazines that will give you the latest information as to what "generation next" is thinking and possibly doing with regards to sex. One such magazine, *React*, which is distributed to schools throughout the country, emphasizes a healthy lifestyle, sexual responsibility, and active communication with parents. There are plenty of television movies and after-school specials on weekday afternoons that address these issues. If the Internet is your thing, you can log on to popular sites such as Yahoo, which daily post information on teenagers and their dating habits. All of the sources that I have mentioned will also provide tips and strategies on how to talk to your kids about sex.

Insist that sex education become part of your child's school curriculum. If at all possible, make sure that your child's school allows you to become a partner in the sex education process. Review whatever curriculum they may have, and even sit in on one of the sex education classes to determine the quality of the information and the attitude of the teacher as well. Back in the day when I attended high school, sexual education classes were a joke. They discussed hygiene, where the sex organs are located, and a little about birth control. A proper sexual education should be comprehensive, addressing both the physical and emotional aspects of sexuality. Discuss with the teachers those aspects of sex education that you find to be more important.

You will also find that the more formal approach taken by the schools (the use of textbooks, etc.) can be very helpful in that it can provide a comprehensive education, whereas the parental approach might be a little more hit and miss. You'll notice that this teaming between you and the school will make the process of teaching sexuality much easier.

Recognize the power of peer pressure. As you are in the process of establishing a solid and open communication line with your teen, especially in discussing sex, always recognize that your child is facing powerful peer pressure when it comes to sexuality. In your talks always explore any ideas they many have about sex and how many of those ideas come from their friends. Discuss whether there are pressures regarding sexual activity in order to fit in with friends. And, of course, offer solutions and options that will help your child become an individual and make independent and responsible decisions about sex. If you can, you must become your child's best friend, especially when it comes to sexual education.

Be a united front. Quite often, parents allow one adult partner in the relationship to do all of the talking and educating about sex. Even if the one parent who does the talking is really good at it, this is not the proper approach. If possible, both parents, whether together or separate, should become a team when it comes to talking about sex. In the first place, it gives the child more balanced information, from both an adult male and female perspective. Since much of sex is about relationships, the team effort is a living demonstration of a man and woman working together around issues of sexuality. Finally, both parents can support one another as well as generate different approaches and ideas to working with the child. Sexual education really should be a family activity.

Don't promote double standards. Remember the 1970s movie *The Mack?* He had money, he had the *jewels* (both kinds!), and he had all the women! To many black men and their sons, the Mack *was* the man. The Mack is dead, but his legacy lives on. Come on guys, admit it. When your sons talk about all their girlfriends or bring girls home, you feel really good about it. "That's my son." "The apple doesn't fall far from the tree." "A chip off the old block." "Hey, baby, it's in the genes."

But on the serious side, what message does this convey to our sons. Not a good one. They begin to internalize this praise as positive reinforcement for polygamous relationships (a whole bunch of chicks), and they begin to equate sex with conquest. Now, in the flip side, when your daughters talk about boys or they bring home a new boyfriend, male parents go postal! Our daughters soon begin to think it is wrong or sinful to have relationships with boys. The double standard must stop when we teach sex education, especially for black boys, who through the additional the influence of rap and hip-hop are being taught a lack of respect for females. So parents, especially you dads, whatever you do, please examine your sexist attitudes and behaviors and teach your sons to be respectful of women by discussing the equality of the sexes, and perhaps advocating serial monogamy in dating. And by the way, cut your daughters some slack! Sheesh!

Abstaining Versus Safe Sex

There has been a raging argument in the past few years about whether we should teach our kids to abstain from sex or practice safe sex. Why this has become the question of the decade escapes me. The answer I believe involves common sense. If you think your child is sexually active, then whatever your beliefs or values, sexual education must include learning about safe sex practices first and abstention second. You've got to put out the fire before you start rebuilding the house. On the other hand, if your child has not been sexually active, then you can emphasize the value of abstaining. However, if you want to cover all your bets, then teach both abstention *and* safe sex.

Abstaining is the safest way for your child to stay out of a situation she can't handle. But, if she has to go there, send her in with as much knowledge as possible. It has been my experience that children who learned about sexuality in an open and unbiased manner usually choose abstention. Why? Because sex is not only about love and passion, but also about knowing how to set priorities and act responsibly. If you teach your children to respect others and themselves, they will make the right decision when the time comes. You know the old saying: You can lead a horse to water but you can't make it drink. And you know that I know what happens when you try to force your beliefs on a child—rebellion! You can't make the decision for your kids, but you can teach them to do something better: make the right decision.

To close, as always, keep communication open and let your child know that they can approach you with any questions or conflicts having to do with sex or anything else. And, above all else, no matter how bad the situation (sexual activity, pregnancy, illness, etc.), don't condemn your child. Instead, problem-solve together. That's what smart parenting is all about!

8

BLACK AND BLUE: KIDS AND POLICE

THERE HAS BEEN A LONG, sad history of violence against people of color by authority figures, especially law enforcement. The beatings that Rodney King and Abner Louima suffered at the hands of racist white cops caused such outrage that it spurred protests, marches, and in King's case, rioting.

In the Bronx, Anthony Baez, a young Dominican-American man playing touch football with his brothers and friends, was subjected to an illegal police choke hold that led to his death. All this after the football accidentally hit an unmarked police car and enraged police officer, Francis Livoti, to the point of killing another human being. According to police statistics, 89 percent of those who died in New York Police custody between 1990 and 1994 were African-American or Hispanic.

These and other incidents exposed the raw hatred that is racism, reinforcing the belief held by many blacks that police brutality and racism in this country is as American as apple pie. And our police forces are a stronghold of this hate and racism.

Blacks and Latinos have been judged by the criminal justice system with a higher, tougher, and less forgiving standard than whites. The foot soldiers of the double standards of law enforcement are America's police, who have added a reputation of violence to their already tarnished image of being racists.

Police Brutality and Racism

Though there may be many cops who are not racist, most people would agree, including black police officers, that the majority of cops are. There are many reasons police brutality and racism exist:

- Police departments across the nation have attracted blue-collar or lower-middle-class whites into their ranks. Many of the neighborhoods in which they were raised in and/or live in are rather small-minded communities that are bastions of xenophobia and intolerance. These attitudes are then carried into police work.
- Cops, just like people in other professions, carry unresolved emotional baggage. However, unlike other professionals, they pack guns and enforce the law. Psychological profiles conducted on police officers show that they are often chronically violent individuals who are prone to alcoholism. Not only are they involved in misconduct on the job, they also have conflicts at home, resulting in a higher rate of domestic violence as compared to other professionals. Add to that their enormous amount of occupational stress and danger and you have the potential for disaster.
- A large number of Americans believe that most violent crimes are committed by blacks. Quite naturally, cops, like everyone else, are conditioned into believing that if you are black you are a suspect.
- The training of police cadets has been incomplete and negligent by failing to provide cultural sensitivity and cultural competence issues as part of their education.
- In large cities, law enforcement officials are given wide latitude to fight crime, even if it means violating people's civil rights. In New York, the Civilian Police Review Board is unable to get justice for victims of police brutality, even though a full 79 percent of the people who lodged complaints from January to June 1995 were African-American or Latino (Amnesty International, June 1996).

While many of us (black folks, that is) have been fortunate enough to steer clear of being in confrontations with the police, we are always potential victims, due to circumstances and situations beyond our control, namely being black. This is not just in our imagination. Citing the statistic that black drivers were 4.85 times as likely to be stopped by troopers in New Jersey—where virtually everyone drives over the fifty-five-mile-per-hour speed limit—state Judge Robert Francis ruled in 1996 that the police had a policy of "selective enforcement" by "targeting blacks for investigation and arrest." As an example of this racist practice, New Jersey state troopers have employed a practice called racial "profiling." African Americans joke about being pulled over for D.W.B.: Driving While Black. The practice involves stopping black drivers solely based on race, with the hope of finding drugs.

As part of this practice, in April 1998, two black and two hispanic college basketball players were pulled over by officers on patrol, ostensibly for speeding on the New Jersey Turnpike in Washington Township. The troopers claimed the driver intentionally placed the vehicle in reverse to run them over. By the time the incident was over, troopers had fired eleven shots into their van, wounding three of the passengers, two seriously. The victims and their families believe the officers overreacted because these students are black and hispanic.

If you think this only happens on the streets or highways, think again. You're not much safer at home, due to "no knock" search warrants. Based solely on the word of confidential informants, the police can burst into your home in search of criminal activity. These violent surprise raids, which utilize tear gas, drawn guns, and riot maneuvers, have traumatized many innocent African-American families. As a political move to bring about damage control, the police apologize when the victims are found to be innocent, but little is being done to actually change police misconduct.

Your Child Could Be Next

Believe it or not, even children, primarily African-American children, are also in peril of being the victims of police brutality. There have been many incidents in which black youngsters were stopped by the police for walking in the "wrong" (usually white) neighborhood. Incredibly, in New York, a black teenager who had dreams of one day becoming a police officer came to the rescue of a cop being attacked by someone he was trying to arrest. The cop recognized the good samaritan's color but not his heroic intentions, and shot him in the leg, thinking he too was the enemy.

This heroic teenager, who tried to do the right thing, is someone's son, and if it could happen to him it could happen to your child. As long as racism and police brutality exist, no matter how much we try to shelter black children, they will always be potential victims of abuse at the hands of the police.

Smart Strategies for Your Child

As part of my clinical practice, I have been called upon to consult and testify in many high-profile police brutality cases that were based on race. I also provided crisis intervention to the victims, who were black and Latino, for their resulting emotional trauma. In addition, I have counseled many police and corrections officers, sent by their employee assistance programs, who have experienced bouts of uncontrollable anger, rage, and other psychological problems. Through these experiences I have developed insight into what the typical cop on the street is thinking, and have created simple but effective strategies that can minimize any confrontation that may happen between your child and the police. For all of the reasons I have discussed, these strategies should be drilled into every African-American child, boy or girl. It truly is a matter of life or death.

Street cops typically misinterpret any assertive behavior as being a challenge and threat to their authority and safety, and that will trigger paranoid, aggressive, and eventually abusive behavior. In other words, if your kid is detained by a cop and is not properly prepared to deal with a possible confrontational situation, he won't stand a chance if things go sour.

Therefore, the goal of these strategies is to defuse, stop, or even prevent a potentially dangerous situation from taking place. Communicating this information to your child is essential smart parenting. Here are rules of conduct in the presence of law enforcement that you must drill into your child:

1. Never, ever, run from a police officer, especially after you have been told to stop and not move.

2. Do not make any sudden moves or gestures in the presence of any cop, even one who is not paying any attention to you. Cops have been trained to react to any sudden gesture or movement as a threat to their physical person and will react with deadly force. Therefore, explain every physical move you are making. For example, "Officer Jones, I am reaching into my back pocket to pull out my ID."

3. If you are being placed under arrest, do not fight or resist the police. They will become angrier, resulting in your being subdued quickly and violently. Many people have been severely injured or accidentally killed in this manner.

4. Always address the police by their title, such as "Officer." Try to read his nameplate and address him as "Officer" in addition to his last name. This tactic will force him to act as a person and not just a "cop." You should also respond to his questions by saying, "Yes, sir," and "No, sir." This will convey a sign of respect on your part. He will immediately feel less challenged.

5. Even if you are scared or angry, stay calm and always be polite, even if the cop is being rude and verbally abusive. Never raise your voice in speaking with a police officer. Always speak in a soft or monotone voice. This will keep the conflict from escalating, and the cop may get the impression that he is dealing with a nice kid. Also, he will not have to raise his voice or level of aggression to maintain a sense of superiority or authority.

6. Don't talk too much. Answer only the questions that you are asked. You can explain your behavior, but do not make any confessions. Remember, whatever you say can be used against you later.

7. Try to commit to memory everything that has happened during the encounter with the police. In the same vein, never ask or demand a name or badge number. Again, commit it all to memory. Cops usually interpret this assertive questioning as a direct threat to their authority. So, as soon as you can, in a safe place away from the police, write down everything that has transpired from memory.

8. Request as quickly as possible that the police officer call or

contact your parents or school. You will need backup and support as quickly as the cops do. As soon as your parents arrive, keep quiet and let them handle the situation.

Strategies for Parents

Parents, there are a few things that you will need to do in order to assist your child through such a potentially dangerous situation.

1. As soon as you arrive on the scene, whether it is in the street or in the station house, don't be overly friendly, volunteering information to the authorities. It may be used against your child later on. Instead, stay calm and businesslike. If you can, arrive with a lawyer or paralegal in tow. The police may not like it, but they will treat you with respect.
2. Just as you've instructed your child to do, commit everything to memory and keep a log of what happens, when and where it happens along with any details you can recall. As time changes so do memories, so do this as the events are happening. Keep it all accurate. Also, request a copy of all paperwork on your child.
3. Even if the situation is resolved to your satisfaction, consult a lawyer as soon as possible. While in the station house, do not sign any documents without first consulting with an attorney. Do not waste time going to the civilian complaint review board unless advised by your attorney. Most of these bodies have no power in addressing abusive behavior by the police.
4. No matter how angry you may be with your child for getting into this type of situation, show family solidarity in front of the cops. Deal with personal issues at home. What you don't want to do is convey any message that your child is deserving of punishment. The cops will take this sentiment and run with it, resulting in more aggressive behavior against your child.
5. As soon as you get out of the Dodge and back home, sit down with your child and talk about the experience. You both will need to vent your feelings about this madness. If the family has also been traumatized, consult not just your lawyer, but

also a mental health professional. If you don't talk about it, the emotional repercussions can be dire. We're talking depression, anxiety, flashbacks, and sleeping and eating problems. Psychologists refer to these symptoms as PTSD, post traumatic stress disorder.

An Ounce of Prevention

As always, an ounce of prevention is worth a pound of cure. If you really want to lower the odds of your child becoming the next beating victim at the hands of a cop, there are political and community options at your disposal. You can lobby your political representatives to increase the budget of the community policing projects in your neighborhoods. Just as important, get to know the police officers in the community relations department of your local precinct. Get these cops involved in activities with our children, such as sponsoring health fairs, drug abuse education, and safety seminars. This will insure more familiarity and sensitivity in dealing with kids and other members of the community. When cops get to know us as real people, they are much better at treating us with the respect we deserve.

Finally, support the efforts of black police fraternal organizations such as the Guardians or One Hundred Black Men in Law Enforcement, who have regional branches in different parts of the nation. These groups work to bring greater cultural sensitivity and stamp out racism in police departments across America.

The real deal is that until law enforcement agencies confront their racist attitudes, black children will always be their next potential beating victims, and for our kids, that's no way to grow up. We all wish things were different, and some progress is being made through the efforts of our communities and different organizations. But until things change, we have to play it smart. Through smart parenting you can show your kids how to successfully walk away from a potentially explosive situation that could otherwise have a tragic ending.

9

TEEN REBELLION

THERE'S NO PLACE TO HIDE. It turns beautiful children into monsters. It changes the family and the home into a war zone. It makes you say terrible things that you always regret later. Oh man, it's downright scary!

We're talking *teen rebellion,* and like the call of the wild, that's right, the call of nature, it's inevitable. This is the tornado with which our teens struggle through the rite of passage from childhood to young adulthood, and though their behaviors are usually to the extreme, you know, a little to the left of outrageous, many of our kids make it through unscathed, even if it means that we as parents end up with posttraumatic stress syndrome. On the other hand, there are many black children from good homes who unfortunately do not make it through the teen rebellion stage, often becoming serious behavior problems. Ultimately, they run afoul of authority and the law, incurring criminal records that mark them for life, putting them squarely on the road to failure.

Their own self-destructive and foolish behaviors aside, there are three major factors which contribute to black children becoming involved in teen rebellion and getting into lots of trouble. They are:

1. *The peer group.* Peer pressure is perhaps one of the most powerful influences that teens face on a day-to-day basis. A

teenager's behavior will often be governed by a need to fit in with the crowd. To be accepted as being hip or cool often translates into behaving or even dressing like the group. This does not allow for much individuality or independence. This is a phase that almost all teenagers go through. However, problems arise when the peer group is composed of teens who have psychological and family problems that cause them to rebel and run afoul of the law. Naturally, the well-mannered teen, in order to keep up with and please the crowd, will also begin to participate in rebellious and sometimes destructive behavior. To make matters worse, if this teen is lacking in self-esteem he may be much more susceptible to negative peer influences due to a lack of inner strength and confidence, which is part of being an individual and having independent thinking.

2. *The media.* Because television, music, and other forms of media seem to glorify the "gangsta" and thug life, it becomes easier for our children to believe that engaging in these defiant behaviors are an acceptable part of establishing their transition from adolescence to the late teen and early adult years.

3. *Prejudice in the legal system.* There is an unequal justice system in America, where black children are arrested for misdemeanors at a much higher rate than their white counterparts. At a recent training I conducted for the Department of Juvenile Justice in Orlando, Florida, parole and probation officers vented their frustration about the extraordinarily high number of caseloads involving African-American children, many arrested for minor violations. White children were almost nonexistent on these same caseloads because when they were caught committing the same violations as the black kids, they were typically escorted home to their parents with no arrests. This example clearly points out that black kids, even those from middle-class homes, are not often given a second chance when they mess up. When white kids rebel, society views them as going through a phase; when black kids rebel, they are classified as delinquents with conduct disorders and incur prison records.

Because of these three factors, it is imperative that we view teen rebellion as normal on the one hand, but a potential disaster to the future of our teens on the other. Black children experiencing teen rebellion do not realize they have a lot more to lose than their white contemporaries. Parents, you have no choice. The cost is evident. You must take responsibility for saving your children and guiding them safely through teen rebellion.

The Family Is Affected, Too

Although it is easy to view teen rebellion as being the problem of the teenager alone, in almost every instance the family is also extremely affected by this very turbulent time. Once peaceful alliances between members of the family are redefined into conflicted and troublesome relationships. Likewise, family members no longer regard each other as thinking and feeling people, but more as one-dimensional characters consigned to negative rolls. The typical family constellation might look something like this: The rebelling daughter or son becomes the "bad seed" or the "child from hell," and mom and dad become the "enforcers," or "judge and jury." With these new roles, you can imaging how once warm relationships become stretched to the breaking point, while communication eventually becomes nonexistent. It's like the kids are from Mars and the parents are from Hackensack.

To better understand, cope, and successfully deal with this difficult time, let's take a closer look at what causes teen rebellion and how smart parenting can help.

What's Goin' On?

During the teenage years a child makes the transition from adolescence (the onset of puberty when sexual maturation begins) to young adulthood. They take the first steps into young adulthood and therefore have many new responsibilities and major life decisions, such as whether and where to attend college. Taking those first steps toward adulthood also has many pitfalls. Mistakes are made and behavior can become outrageous. This is a result of being under mommy and daddy's wing or, with some kids, under their thumbs for so long that they push the envelope on getting freedom. For most kids, freedom means following your own mind, making your own decisions, and thinking and expressing your own thoughts. However, too often a teenager's "own thoughts" seem to be anything that is 180 degrees opposite of what their parents say or believe. It means examining and challenging all the rules laid down or taught by parents in order to see what fits and discarding what doesn't. It's the discarding part that parents often interpret as challenges to authority.

Parents tend to become fearful of the situations that accompany their teen's physical, emotional, and sexual maturation. They often respond by becoming overprotective and trying to clamp down on their children's efforts at freedom. In turn, oppositional behavior expressed by the teens is fueled by hormonal changes, with peer pressure thrown in for good measure, resulting in buck-wild behaviors influenced by the Malcolm X approach—"By any means necessary." Of course, this is when everything goes haywire, the family explodes, the teens are out of control, and the parents book a second honeymoon to Bellevue Psychiatric.

Whoa! Let's calm down a minute. What we need to understand is that teenage rebellion is a normal part of growing up. No matter the behavior—good, bad, or somewhere in between—our kids are not bad seeds. Teen rebellion is a legitimate struggle whereby children define themselves as individuals, different from their siblings, and especially different from their parents. With smart parenting, our goal should be to keep the rebellious behavior from crashing out of bounds, helping our teens through one of the most difficult times in their lives.

Manifestations of Teen Rebellion

Teens will seek to define themselves as young and independent adults in a variety of ways. Some of these expressions are rebellious but they are harmless, while other behaviors are more serious, with harmful effects possibly reaching far into their futures.

Fashion

Style or fashion is certainly one expression of identity, and an innocuous one at that. You know that look right now—baggy jeans, designer leather jackets, and brand name sneakers. Doesn't it seem that the more upset we get with them for wearing these fashions the happier they are? Well, that's why they do it. This style of clothing is totally foreign to parents and therefore uniquely their own. A real problem does exist, however, when our kids believe that these types of items bring high status. If they don't have the newest Timberland jacket, Air Jordan sneaker, or some other designer item, they don't think they will be part of the in crowd. As we all know, there are teens who become desperate enough that if they don't have the money to buy these items, they will simply steal them. This is the kind of behavior that gets them into trouble with the law.

Rap

Just as white kids worship rock, grunge, or heavy metal music, so black kids have embraced rap. Gangsta rap is considered by many parents and social scientists to be the major negative influence on the lives of young African Americans. In fact, rap music defines "generation next"; it is their voice, and its bad-boy image has become their anthem. Because this is a vitally important topic, I have devoted a whole chapter to rap and its effects on black youth (Chapter 10). When you're ready, just take a walk into the hip-hop zone.

Sex

Many teens believe they are engaging in adult behavior that is mature, but for them it is actually inappropriate and possibly self-destructive and rebellious, such as sex. To be an older teen, especially a boy, and still be a virgin is not considered cool. Because of AIDS and the higher incidence of other sexually transmitted diseases, more kids than ever before are starting to consider abstinence. Even so, a lot of teens still engage in sexual activity, often for the wrong reasons, and sometimes with calamitous effects.

Failing in School

Especially in the African-American community, kids who were once academically strong are now flunking out of school in record numbers. I can't tell you how many parents come to see me in desperation because their children are doing poorly in school. For many of these kids, to do badly in school is their way of making an antiestablishment statement. Peer pressure causes them to think that getting good grades is a fate relegated to nerds and herbs: "Yo kid, you got another ninety in math! You try'n' to be white or somethin'?"

Despite all of our strides in civil rights, it's both sad and ironic that many of our teens do not understand that education is the only key to independence. This is one type of rebellious behavior that you must take steps to address—or your child may miss the boat.

Parents Contribute, Too

As your child approaches young adulthood, it can be both exciting and terrifying for you as a parent. You see your son or daughter beginning to venture toward more adult and complex situations. Adding stress to this situation is the frightening state of the world. The threats to children are many. These dangers are not just on the streets, but even in the assumed safety of our homes, where children can be lured into sexual assaults through the Internet. As black parents, we are especially afraid because of the hostile physical and psychological environments African-American children face. There is an alarming rate of black-on-black crime, and, let's face it, quite often our neighborhoods are not the safest.

Many parents freak out from this type of stress and try to control the uncontrollable by restricting their kids' behaviors. There have been more cases in the news lately of parents who, in frustration and desperation to control their out-of-control children, have handcuffed them to their apartment radiators!

Of course, most restrictive parental approaches ultimately backfire. The kids become frustrated and angry, rebelling even more. The parents in turn become less tolerant, turn up the heat, and—boom!—an explosive family situation erupts.

Since almost all teenagers experience some sort of rebellion, it is important to assess your teen's degree of risk for self-destructive, dangerous, or antisocial behavior as part of teen rebellion. With this knowledge you can determine the severity of the situation as well as the type or level of intervention needed. Your teen will most likely fall into one of the following levels of rebellion.

The Three Levels of Rebellion

Mild Rebellion

A teen in mild rebellion will misbehave in ways that do not cause the teen to become much of a behavior problem in the home or school. He might stay out past curfew or cut classes on occasion. There is some experimentation with smoking and drinking. Sexual activity usually begins. There are occasional arguments with parents. Funky fashions and clothes dictate his dressing style.

Even if your child is only at the level of mild rebellion, *don't* go to sleep on it! Your child's behavior should still be monitored and addressed before it progresses to a higher level.

Moderate Rebellion

At this level, there is a great deal more negative or bad behavior in the home and at school. House rules are more easily questioned and broken. There is more truancy from school and grades begin to drop. There is usually more frequent negative contact with authority figures and even possibly with the law. There is also more drug and alcohol use, as well as a significant amount of anger, which is expressed through aggressive behavior such as fighting with other teens or membership in gangs.

Severe Rebellion

Can you say Black Caesar? At this level, we have teenagers who have built a wall between themselves and most adults, including teachers, parents, and any other authority figures. There is almost always gang membership. Quite often these kids carry guns or other weapons not only for defense but also for bravado. Many of these teens see a jail term as a badge of honor. Selling or using drugs is also an active part of their lives, and sexual activity becomes reckless.

Building Character

If you have a good understanding of what teen rebellion is all about, hopefully you will take it less personally and be able to concentrate more on helping your teen make this important transition from adolescence to adulthood. I personally believe it is essential for you to be there for your teenager, because the struggle and turmoil experienced at this stage of life separates the men from the boys and the women from the girls. What I mean by this is that teen rebellion is a rite of passage. For a teen the act of successfully negotiating through these years, especially with your help, can strengthen character. Therefore, your interactions with your kids around the issues of rebellion should be focused, reductional, supportive, and inspirational. This is one of the most critical times when your child is really going to need a parent *and* a friend. And you, my dear parents, are going to need a lot of help in accomplishing this difficult feat.

That's why I offer you Emotional Rescue: Dr. Jeff's Eight Steps to Helping Your Teen Rebel Constructively. Through thousands of my therapy sessions, these strategies evolved to rescue even the most hardened teens whose behaviors were booking them first-class tickets to jail. These techniques have brought together families that were being torn apart by conflict.

As you are reading the following strategies, keep in mind that you must be consistent in your approach. You've got to do this stuff every day. Second, these strategies work better when parents work as a team. If both parents are in the house, then work together. If you are separated or divorced, put your issues aside. Get together as often as you can, as friends and parents, to discuss how you can work as a united front. If you are a single parent, then you must work doubly hard at it.

Dr. Jeff's Eight Steps to Helping Your Teen Rebel Constructively

1. Pick Your Battles

We must learn to weed out the small problems from the large and concede the less important battles. Resist giving criticism on every issue and save the firm stands for the really big problems. For example, why make a federal case out of your kid's staying out past curfew, especially if she's only late by fifteen minutes? However, if she violates curfew several times in a month and it is becoming a chronic problem, then, by all means, she should be called on the carpet. Instead, if you choose to make a big deal out of every transgression, there will be no end to conflict and arguments, which in turn will lead to more resentment and acting out by your teenager.

Jacques' parents picked on him for everything—at least that's the way he saw it. Jacques was a first-generation American, his parents having emigrated from Trinidad. And as is typical of many Caribbeans, his parents were quite strict. They complained about his baggy pants, his choice of music (he loved Wycliff and the Fugees), his friends, and, of course, his failing grades. The conflicts continued to mount, and as Jacques grew more frustrated with his parents his behavior became worse. In family therapy, we were getting nowhere fast. Finally, I had his parents write a list of the things they found objectionable about his behavior. Then I had them prioritize the objectionable behaviors. They soon came to realize that most of the issues were not that bad, but just a matter of personal style, not rebellion. His grades emerged as the most salient issue. We then concentrated on this issue and let everything else go. Since Jacques then felt he had more breathing room to be himself and make his own decisions in most areas of his life, he became more amenable to improving his schoolwork. His grades soared, and he came to appreciate his parents' flexibility and good sense in focusing on only the most important issue.

Now you try it.

On a piece of paper, list all of your kid's problem behaviors. For example:

She stays out past curfew.
She refuses to do her chores.
She misses a few days of school per month for no reason.
She keeps her room like a pigsty and refuses to clean it up.
She wears outlandish clothes.
She smokes cigarettes after school with her friends.

Next, prioritize the list from least destructive to most destructive. The least destructive are behaviors that you might be able to live with at least temporarily. Usually they are not causing long-term physical harm and have not influenced family relationships, scholastic work, and achievement in general. The most destructive behaviors, on the other hand, threaten all aspects of functioning and relationships.

Begin addressing the most destructive and bothersome behaviors right away, and let up on the least dangerous. Once the real problems are identified there's less emotional clutter, and you can be more focused on addressing your teen's issues. Chances are that once you resolve the more serious behaviors the least important ones will cease...or cease to be important.

2. Initiate Real Two-way Communication With Your Teen

Of course, you're thinking: How can anyone communicate with these knuckleheaded kids? It can be done, and there are some easy and novel ways of doing this. The most effective approach is to interact with them on their turf, in their space. This means hanging out and joining them in some of their favorite activities or pasttimes. The goal is to get your teen more comfortable and less uptight in opening up to you. In this more relaxed atmosphere (home field advantage) you can talk about their daily activities and what sorts of conflicts they may be involved in with friends or even authority figures. For example:

- Watch music videos together.
- Play video games with your teen on the Sony Play Station and discuss play strategies. (At first he'll beat the pants off of you, but you should eventually survive to win a point or two.)
- Go out to a basketball game to see his favorite player or team. If you can't afford that, watch the game on television, and make popcorn or other refreshments. No, they can't have any Old English 800!
- Though you can do all the above activities with sons and daughters alike, for the girls specifically, you may want to attend a concert with her favorite teen idol, or go out shopping together for clothes or CDs.

- Most important, keep the hot air out of your stomach and the wax out of your ears and be willing to listen. Quite often we parents are too busy lecturing and don't allow kids the room or time to explain their feelings. We may think we're saying something profound, but believe me, all they are hearing is—"blah, blah, blah"!

3. Be a Positive Role Model

During the teenage rebellion years, you will be challenged to work with your teen around some explosive issues. At times your patience will be pushed to the limit, especially because communication usually breaks down during this stage. As long as you keep your cool and don't lose your temper, you can deal with a crisis with your teen. A 1998 *New York Daily News* survey found that over 70 percent of teenagers consider their parents to be the most influential forces in their lives. Therefore it is incumbent on you to not only listen and give good advice, but to do it in a calm and rational manner. If you want your teen to use problem-solving skills when dealing with their conflicts, you have got to set an example and do the same. If you "talk the talk" you better "walk the walk."

4. Never Make a Decision When Angry

Some of the most tragic and accidental cases of child abuse occur when a parent is angry and disciplining a child at the same time. Not only does the child become totally fearful or equally angry, the disciplinary lesson is lost and, even worse, the parent can injure the child. Also, it's common knowledge that we often misinterpret situations when angry and blow them out of proportion. Therefore, as parents we should try as much as humanly possible to address our kids' rebellious or outrageous behaviors in a rational and calm manner. You can utilize the following steps to discipline your teen without anger:

- Do whatever it takes to calm down. Count to ten, take a walk, or listen to relaxing music. Just leave it alone for the moment.
- While you are starting to chill, let your kid know that the rebellious behavior in question *will* be revisited later in the day (you don't want "Junior" to think he's getting away with the behavior).

- Conduct your own investigation of the situation. Interview the other kids or people involved. This way, you'll be armed with the facts.
- If need be, bring in an objective third party as a voice of reason. The other parent or close relative usually fits the bill pretty well.
- Seek advice from other parents who have been through similar situations. Their experiences will give you valuable information and suggestions, and let you known that you are not alone. There are a lot of other parents who are in your shoes. That fact alone will make you feel much better!

When finally speaking with your teen, continue to stay cool, calm, and collected. State your piece and allow your teen to state his. The two of you should establish a forum for discussing issues that may come up in the future. For example, set aside a weekly block of time where you both can address issues that your teen is facing at home or in the world. For the most part, problems will be discussed and solved before they reach a crisis.

5. Expose Your Teen to More Positive Peer Groups

We should never underestimate the importance of peer groups in the lives of our children. In many respects, peer groups often contribute and are supportive of teen rebellion. How often do we complain about our kids hanging out with the "wrong crowd"? According to our kids, however, their friends can do no wrong. If you try to separate your kids from their friends, quite often they will embrace them even more. When it comes to separating them from their cronies, you could more easily remove a brain tumor with a dull scalpel!

Instead, use the "back door approach" by introducing or exposing your kids to a more positive peer group. Then at least they get to make up their own minds about who their new friends or acquaintances will be.

You're now probably thinking, "Where do I find these so-called positive peer groups?" It's easy. These types of kids play team sports, are involved in the arts, and are part of civic organizations. So the best way of connecting your kids to this group is by having them attend, on a trial basis, after-school activities such as the school newspaper, orchestra, choir, or team sports. One of these activities should catch their attention and interest. If that doesn't happen, then use smart parenting to give them an incentive. For example, if they attend one of these activities regularly they can get that new mini-disc system, the latest Play Station, or whatever you both decide on. If you can keep them interested, eventually they will participate in the after-school activity just for pure enjoyment and pleasure. They will hopefully begin to form new and positive friendships, and you will soon notice positive changes in their behavior.

By the way, you can kill two birds with one stone. Much rebellious teen behavior grows out of teen boredom. The idle mind truly is a playground for the Devil. Being involved in extracurricular activities will keep teens occupied and productive.

6. Encourage Your Teen to Take On More Responsibilities

The problem with many of our teens is that they simply have it too easy. Rarely do they have to earn anything on their own. This, of course, leads to a lack of moral fiber and backbone. In our zeal to give our kids a better life than what we had, we end up spoiling them. They, in turn, begin to believe that the world is their oyster and often rebel when they don't get what they want. During their teen years, this type of behavior becomes even more exaggerated and dangerous. In this case, a part-time job can be a particularly positive experience that can also relieve boredom, teach skills, provide confidence, increase self-esteem, and, most importantly, build character. Also, earning a wage will keep your child from finding or even entertaining illegal ways to attain money.

If your child does not have a job, then make sure he is assigned and completes a moderate number of weekend or daily chores around the house. There is nothing wrong with paying your child to do the chores as long as he really earns the money by doing a good job. Chores have the added benefit of instilling structure and creating self-discipline.

Adam's middle name was trouble. He grew up in a privileged family in which his parents gave him everything. As soon as he hit his teen years, he was demanding and out of control. He wouldn't listen to anyone, least of all his parents. He was the proverbial spoiled brat. Two years of individual and family therapy seemed to only cause Adam and his parents more conflict. One afternoon, right after another stormy therapy session, I asked Adam to copy and collate a manuscript I had completed. I was short-staffed, desperate, and needed the manuscript to be delivered within the hour. To my and his parents' amazement, Adam came through with flying colors. He finally exhibited control and responsibility. Seizing on this breakthrough, I got him a part-time job as a clerk with another clinic. This new responsibility did wonders for his maturity and impulse control. Shortly thereafter, our therapy sessions became more productive, and Adam and his family worked out significant long-standing issues.

7. Give Lots of Positive Reinforcement and Encouragement

Just think about it. Everything you are, everything you do, is supported by encouragement and reward. Whether it is a promotion for a job well done or making enough money to keep food on the table, we all need to be rewarded for our behavior. The same goes for our teens. Earlier in the book we discussed positive reinforcement as a way for younger kids to develop self-esteem. By the time these kids become teenagers they will face new assaults on their self-esteem. That's why you will need to give positive reinforcement and encouragement as much as ever! Any productive behavior, large or small, should be praised. This can include when they clean their bedroom, throw out the garbage, mow the lawn, return the videos, do the laundry or dishes, read a novel from the library, go from a C to a B in a class, help a sibling do homework, attend an after-school activity, and on and on. Believe me, they will feel good about the praise and continue to perform good deeds to get more.

8. Seek Psychological or Medical Help If Your Child Is Out of Control

As mentioned earlier, rebellious behavior may be the result of some emotional or physical problem. This may include something as mild as a learning disorder or something as serious as clinical depression. A child with attention deficit hyperactivity disorder has trouble focusing, paying attention, and/or sitting still, among other symptoms which can be misinterpreted as willful bad behavior. In addition, because the teen usually cannot control these symptoms without therapeutic intervention, she soon begins to believe that she is a misbehaving, disruptive person. Proper diagnosis by a health professional and timely intervention will not only improve the problem, but also save you and your teenager a lot of frustration and conflict if you know what battle you are really fighting.

Finally, keep in mind that some behaviors, especially drug dependent behaviors, may be partly genetic. If you have a family history of drug dependency, then your teenager may also be at risk for the same problem. Keeping this in mind will also lead you to seek early intervention at the first sign of trouble.

If you try these eight steps with your kids, you'll see that they make a lot of sense, even though it is hard work. Things might get worse before they get better, but I guarantee that the hard work will pay off. You'll definitely lose some of the battles, but will be much more likely to win the war. Don't despair, because if you give up you'll only further hurt your child. Don't expect changes overnight, but work to maintain constant, steady communication with your teen. If you work at it, the results will undoubtedly be much better than if you walk away and ignore the situation. At the end of the day, remember that you brought your teenager this far, so you must be doing something right! Just keep up the good work!

10

THE HIP-HOP ZONE

LISTEN UP! Are the names Puff Daddy, Busta Rhymes, Mary J. Blige and L. L. Cool J so common in your home you feel you should be charging them rent? Do posters of these folks and others (some resembling thugs) wearing "do-rags," $150 sneakers, and pants hanging halfway off their butts adorn your kids' rooms? Do deafening bass lines pounding from your kid's boom boxes rattle your kitchen pots and pans, and shake your mother-in-law's fine china?

Is that an affirmative? Well, my dear parents, you have clearly entered the hip-hop zone—a world where jive-talkin', booty-shakin' crooners, rappers, and deejays are setting trends and defining today's generation next and the lives they live!

By now you may ha-10ve realized that the hip-hop world heavily influences your children's present and future. People, we're talking the whole "shebang" here: jailhouse clothes, slang language, "bad" attitudes, diss-y behavior, and even the gangsta-like friends they have. So, the sixty-four-thousand-dollar question in the minds of millions of parents and the focus of this chapter: Is hip-hop culture good or bad?

This question is an important one particularly to African Americans, not only because the hip-hop culture evolves from and feeds off the urban black experience, but because the hip-hop "playas" are predominantly black. As a result, African-

American children more easily identify with and idolize these characters and are more influenced by the music and their behavior.

"Bad Boys, Bad Boys, What'cha Gonna Do?"

Our fears are not eased any by the fact that hip-hop continues to project a "bad boy" image based on the law-breaking, trouble-making behavior of some of its most popular rap personalities. Dennis Coles, a.k.a. Ghostface Killah, of the Wu-Tang Clan was busted by the New York Police Department for wearing a bullet-proof vest and carrying a .357 Magnum loaded with hollow-point bullets. He has already been charged with robbery for an unrelated crime.

But this is just the tip of the iceberg. A month earlier, Wu-Tang Clan member Russel Jones, a.k.a. Ol Dirty Bastard, was charged in New York with beating his wife and being a deadbeat dad. In 1994 he was shot in the stomach over an argument about rap music. Another member, Clifford Smith, a.k.a. Method Man, was arrested for assaulting a security guard.

In a disturbing new trend, black journalists, especially those who work for magazines that cover the rap and hip-hop world, have begun complaining of threats and physical attacks by irate rappers. It seems that these rappers feel that they have been dissed by negative reviews written by the journalists. At other times they are upset for not making the covers of the magazines. In a recent case, Jesse Washington, the editor in chief of *Blaze*, a rap magazine, said that in an act of retribution, he was stomped in the face and struck with chairs by four men, two he recognized as being rap producers.

This very violent side of hip-hop and rap has the potential to lead black kids into disaster, as it romanticizes the thug life, that is, a lifestyle of drinking "40s," smoking weed, and engaging in drive-by shootings. Also, according to this way of life, members of the opposite sex are referred to as "ho's" and "bitches," whose only purpose is to provide sex on demand for "the fellas." Is it any wonder it becomes terrifying for parents when they know their kids idolize this music, especially when their children are beginning to experiment with negative or rebellious behavior?

Is this lifestyle promoted by the music or by the bad boys themselves? I believe it is promoted by a combination of both. The bad boys don't actually tell kids "Do as I do" or "Do as I say," but the lyrics say, "I got my forty [beer], I got my dope, and I got my 'bitch,' now I'm ready to party," and then the rapper gets busted for smoking pot, using drugs, drinking, and beating women! Kids who listen to the music and idolize the messenger have to be influenced by both the music and the behavior of the messenger. It's a double dose. As parents and a community, we cannot afford to ignore this issue if we are to guide our children and give them the knowledge to empower them to success and personal greatness.

In our quest to find an answer to this all-consuming question of whether rap is good or bad, let's first sort out the predominant issues and concepts of hip-hop, their effects on our society, and, more importantly, on our children. At the same time, we can also gain a better understanding of the realities our children confront and live with. Eventually we can use this information as part of smart parenting to improve communication with our kids and even influence their behavior.

Rap Was First, Now Let There Be Hip-hop

First off, let's define hip-hop, especially since many of you may be unable to tell the difference between hip-hop, rap, and "gangsta."

Rap emerged on the scene with pioneer artists such as Curtis Blow, Run DMC, and Grand Master Flash and the Furious 5. Their catchy "raps"—words spoken to funky music—hit on the experiences of the streets, whether it be hard living in the ghetto or fun times partying with friends till dawn.

Hip-hop grew out of rap. It combines singing with the raps. Many rap stars now rap and sing on their hip-hop records, the most notable these days being Queen Latifah. The term *hip-hop* has become a universal catch-phrase for rap, funk, and R&B recorded by young artists, both male and female. While much of rap music is heavy on the daily, slice-of-life experiences of inner-city youth, hip-hop shows a picture of the hopes and realities and all the experiences, good and bad, of today's urban and suburban youth, such as falling in love for the first time, losing a lover, resisting the lure of sex and drugs, or even lamenting the death of a friend from violence.

East Coast Versus West Coast

In the past few years there's been a rather well-publicized rivalry between rappers from opposite coasts, much to the secret delight of the recording industry, whose sales seem to increase following infamous incidents and the untimely deaths of rap stars.

East Coast music is composed and recorded primarily in New York, while the center for West Coast music is Los Angeles, where many of the rappers are homegrown in Compton. As for the real difference between East Coast and West Coast? Forget the hype—here's the real deal. While the East Coast music paints vivid and often disturbing pictures of urban teen life, a life punctuated by emotional struggle and isolation, West Coast rap has focused on and developed an unhealthy reputation for glorifying gangs and has come to be known as gangsta rap, because Los Angeles, Oakland, and neighboring communities have always had more gangs than other large metropolitan areas on the West Coast.

Some social scientists, educators, and concerned parents believe hip-hop music and its images have been responsible for the interest and surge in gang membership among African-American youth in the past three years on the East Coast and other large cities outside of Los Angeles. Why? The music makes it seem cool to be in a gang. It conveys the message that gang membership offers excitement, status, power, and camaraderie, and that you need gang membership to survive the streets. For instance, 2Pac Shakur and Snoop Doggy Dog rapped about gangs being a way of life and necessary for survival on the streets in their early music.

Meanwhile, the rivalry between East Coast and West Coast music has resulted in some very deadly tragedies. It has been rumored, for example, that rappers such as Notorious B.I.G. (Christopher Wallace), 2Pac (Tupac Shakur), and Death Row Records founder Suge Knight were recording music by day and involved in gang activity by night. In fact, the murders of Biggie and 2Pack are being investigated as gang hits related to the East Coast versus West Coast wars for the financial control of the rap and hip-hop industry.

"We Have a Message in Our Music"

It would be unfair to view the majority of hip-hop as being destructive or merely a representation of thug life. It also would be a mistake not to look beyond the surface level of the messages of the music, where we can see the concerns of our children.

Hip-hop artist L'il Kim, a new 1990s sex symbol, portrays the image of a promiscuous bad girl mainly due to her outrageous G-string outfits, provocative posing, and X-rated raps. Although it would be very easy to condemn her as promoting and encouraging kids to engage in promiscuous sex, there is another message, if we care enough to listen. And we must; because our kids are listening. L'il Kim also talks about having safe sex! And even though we may want our sons and daughters to abstain from sex or wait until they're older, we also want them to be empowered and prepared for the responsibilities of having sex. So listening to her music and following her advice may not be that bad after all. As the mighty O'Jays sang, "We Have a Message in Our Music," you better believe that today's hip-hop artists also carry very powerful messages in their music!

The messages, in fact, give parents a window into the souls of their children, providing an intimate look into their world. Through this music we can discover the things they respect, the nuances of their slang, the styles of the times, and their attitudes and outlook on life. Do you really think you can afford *not* to listen to this music? I don't think you can.

You want a second opinion? The University of California at Berkeley is teaching the message in the music. It is now offering a course called Tupac Shakur 101, a serious and scholarly review of Shakur's music as a reflection of the urban experience. His messages are real, and maybe you should study his lyrics, not only because they may affect your children, but also because they may tell you about their secret lives.

Hip-hop Role Models

To their credit, many hip-hop artists recognize that their messages influence the behavior of our youngsters, and some, including Salt and Peppa, Queen Latifah, KRS-1, and Will Smith have taken the responsibility of sending out clearly positive and socially conscious messages. To many parents, however, they may still offend. But let's face it: Our kids may listen and learn from this music more naturally than they do from the awkward talks we have with them about "the birds and the bees." Kids who are into rap will be more influenced by the message of the music than by what parents have to say. Why not the best of both worlds: Music and parents teaming up for messages aimed at our youth?

Realizing the influence hip-hop has on our children, two Brooklyn social service agencies did just that. Miracle Makers and the Youth Advisory Committee have teamed up to produce a hip-hop video on safe sex and HIV prevention called *Knowledge Is Power*. The New York City Department of Health has provided the major funding for this project, recognizing hip-hop as a direct line into our young people's minds. The target population chosen for this video are young Latino, Haitian, and Caribbean immigrants and their descendants who are most at risk for HIV. In the video, numerous Caribbean hip-hop stars "cipher" (discuss) in Spanish, English, and Haitian Creole the value of safe sex versus unprotected sex ("You gotta have a condom.")

If You Can't Beat 'Em, Join 'Em

Clearly, hip-hop can be either a negative or a positive force in our kids' lives, and we, as parents, must learn how to harness and take advantage of this powerful medium. If you fear that hip-hop has become a major influence in the emotional development of your child, especially a negative one, then, damn it, do something about it! As my Jewish friends always say, "When you get lemons, you make lemonade." In other words, if hip-hop music is everything to your child, then use it as a way to communicate with him in order to change negative attitudes and behaviors.

The bottom line is that hip-hop is not going away anytime

soon, and you can't keep your kids from being exposed to it. So if you use it wisely, it can actually be a positive force in your kids' lives. Let's figure out how to do that.

A few months ago, I received a call from the Bartholomew family. They complained about how their sixteen-year-old daughter, Keisha, went from being a nice model student to being a noncommunicative (at least with her parents), belligerent, Shaqueta-type (you know: bamboo earrings, "stank" attitude, plenty of horizontal neck action) who was obsessed with hip-hop music and videos. The Bartholomews feared that their daughter's morals were being influenced by this music. Her grades plummeted. Not only did she dress provocatively, she began smoking "bities" (East Indian cigarettes that pack a strong buzz) and "rope" (marijuana). And, she began hanging out with boys big time! Their worst fear was that she had become sexually active and might become pregnant, or worse, contract HIV.

After providing Keisha with some individual counseling, I realized that she was strongly influenced by the hip-hop culture, but there was also very strong peer pressure from friends and acquaintances. Yo! She was simply growing up and presenting signs of rebellion, which every teenager experiences to some degree. Her love of hip-hop had been scapegoated by her parents. (Check out Chapter 9 where I discuss the "joys" of Teen Rebellion!) Since they not only failed to effectively communicate with Keisha, they further alienated her by attacking her love of this music. I advised them to take another tack.

The first thing they had to do was to chill out and stop "sweating" her. (This also brought down their blood pressure!) The next step was to find a way to open communication and get into her head or, even better, her heart. What better way to do this than through her love of hip-hop!

The problem was that these parents didn't know the difference between Puff Daddy and Cocoa Puffs. They needed a quick infusion of hip-hop knowledge in order to talk with Keisha about the things that were relevant to her. Their homework assignment was to read hip-hop magazines such as The Source and Vibe, the bibles of hip-hop. They were also required to watch TV shows such as BET's Rap City and Yo MTV Raps. Surprisingly, they actually enjoyed what they read and viewed. They learned more about the hip-hop generation, but most importantly, they were able to learn more about Keisha and her world.

Lo and behold, it worked! Keisha, in turn, opened up to her parents. She learned to respect them more because she appreciated their effort to reach out to her. She eventually changed from a "Shaqueta" to a "Moesha." In all honesty, she did rebel to some degree, but more importantly, she came to listen to her parents more often and subsequently was never in any significant trouble at school or at home.

Some of you may now be saying, "Great story, Dr. Jeff, but hello?! How do we develop whatever skills we have to stimulate conversation and connect to our teenagers?"

Well, my dear parents, fret no more, and don't get your panties in a bunch! Let me give you a couple of simple steps on how to talk to your kids through the funky beat of hip-hop. If you follow these instructions, you will become the envy of friends and neighbors. And, more important, you will become better parents, too! For good or bad (and yes, we will answer this question soon), hip-hop is here to stay, so what follows are five ways to use it to your advantage.

Five Ways to Use Hip-hop to Get Along With Your Child

1. Share Observations About the Hip-hop World

Right before or after family meals, pull out articles in the paper that report on any aspect of the hip-hop community, whether it be an arriving concert, a new hip-hop related TV show, or even a news event on the positive or outrageous behavior of a hip-hop artist. Then open up a discussion with your child. While you may not agree with his position or thinking, at least you're talking about what's important to him. For example, L'il Kim made newspaper headlines when local municipalities were unsuccessful in banning a concert appearance at a stadium in New Jersey because her celebrated X-rated hip-hop and rap shows began at midnight, which violated local cabaret and building code regulations. L'il Kim not only performed, but she started the show around 1:00 A.M. This was an obvious message of defiance to the local authorities.

This news item was loaded with topics that could not only stimulate a conversation but also address and strengthen personal values. Here are a few examples:

Holding your position, fighting for what you think is right
More political or peaceful ways of making a point
Was there racism behind the attempted banning of the concert?
What are some of the messages behind L'il Kim's sexy image?

2. Watch Music Videos With Your Children

Watching videos can also be a good time to talk. Today's videos are often written, produced, and directed quite well. Like the news items in hip-hop magazines, you can discuss many topics, including:

The meaning behind the video
Your child's opinions about the message of the video
How kids can relate the message of the video to their own lives

Discussing rap or hip-hop CDs in the same manner as videos is just as powerful. As I mentioned earlier, the music is a window to the souls of our kids.

Chilly was sent to me for therapy by his parents. It seemed he rarely attended school and was failing. He started smoking a lot of pot, dressed slovenly, and looked like a thug. On his first visit, you could hear him and his music blasting away on the elevator coming up—he was carrying his boom box playing rap and hip-hop music. When I asked him what was up with the music, he said he carried it everywhere. He further stated that he understood the music, and the music spoke to him. His style was loud and so was the music.

Since he did not actively try to communicate with me in our sessions, I let him play the music in my office (but not in my waiting room!). From the music I learned much about him. He would pick selections that expressed the mood he was feeling at the

*time. In order to get him to verbalize, I asked him to write his own
rap lyrics in order to express his pain and anger. That turned out
to be a great release for him. He began to verbalize in therapy and
later with his parents, which he had never done before. I also
recommended to his parents that they seize this opportunity by
following my technique. Chilly has put away his boom box, speaks
for himself, and, incidentally, is a good rapper.*

3. Find the Similarities Between the Music of Today and That of Your Generation

Sit down and share your music and thoughts with your child. In
looking for similarities between your musical passions, you and
your child can begin to develop a deeper understanding of each
other's tastes and hopefully find a common ground to communication and respect. Music and rhythm has always been an
integral part of the African-American community. We must use
this tradition to forge a bond with our kids through the mutual
love of our music in all its forms.

When I was growing up, my parents would play classical
music throughout the house most of the time. I, on the other
hand, would lock myself in my room and listen to music from
such groups as the Beatles, Steppenwolf, and Sly and the
Family Stone. I hated that crusty classical stuff, and my parents
disdainfully described my music as "yeah, yeah, yeah" music.
Not wanting to listen to each other's music actually caused us to
spend more time in opposite ends of the house, separating us
physically and emotionally.

Our situation continued to deteriorate until Armando, a
family friend and an exiled musician from Cuba, came to the
house one afternoon and began banging out some tunes on the
piano. After taking some requests from us, I think he noticed
that we all loved music, but had very different tastes. Armando
decided to play a little trick on us. He improvised a three-
quarter-time classical-sounding waltz to the tune of the Beatles'
"I Wanna Hold Your Hand." My parents didn't immediately
identify the tune but loved it. I quickly realized what was
happening and became fascinated with this melding of classical
and rock music. The bottom line was that my parents and I sat
through and enjoyed classical and rock music together. We

realized the music was different but that it could be very similar, just like our beliefs and tastes. This experience started us on a path toward finding similarities and understanding in other areas of life. Incredibly, my parents later began to let me play pop music throughout the house (my father loved "Baby Love" by the Supremes), and I began to study classical piano.

My own experience helped me create a solution for a father and son who were just not dealing with each other at all.

Malik and his dad were having severe communication problems and wouldn't talk for long periods of time. In a family therapy session, I picked a neutral topic and led them into a discussion of the music they each liked. To no surprise, Malik was a hip-hop fanatic; his dad was a jazz lover. We had animated and sometimes heated discussions of the possible similarities between both musical genres, as well as how the music represented certain feelings, attitudes, and experiences. They both agreed that the music wasn't just melodies but had spiritual significance for each of them. And guess what? Because of this shared belief, in the one session they began talking to each other more than they had in the past six months. This opened the door to more mutual respect and heartfelt conversations on all types of topics. Today Malik and his dad share a closer relationship and sometimes even listen to music together!

If you're wondering how to get together with your kids to listen and share music, here are some simple suggestions:

- While riding in the car together, alternate between hip-hop stations and your favorite music.
- Go shopping for CDs together, and help your kid choose a CD from another musical style that perhaps you enjoy. At home you can listen to the CDs together and discuss their merits.
- When listening to music together at picnics or parties, use a shift system, playing random selections of different styles of music from a variety of CDs. Mix your jazz with hip-hop and see where the conversations go.

4. Use Hip-hop Culture for Quality Time With Your Kid

You know you are always complaining that you don't spend enough time with the kiddies, and even when you do, they're bored out of their skulls. Well, I suggest that you use hip-hop to get next to them. Consider the following tips:

- Take the kids to live concerts. For every hip-hop concert they attend, take them to a jazz or soul/R&B concert.
- Accompany your kids when they go shopping for the latest and "phat-est" hip-hop fashions. What better time to relax and just kick it! Who knows, you might even be able to get them to buy pants that actually fit around the waist. (Hey! Aren't those your old bell-bottoms in the Funky Fashion Department?)

5. Help Your Kid Get Smarter by Reading About Hip-hop Culture

Surprise! Your kids can expand their knowledge through hip-hop. Even though they love the music and known how to "bust the moves" (dance), they can also gain knowledge of current events from hip-hop–related media. At the same time, they can learn how to be critical of what they're absorbing from hip-hop. Additionally, if you want the added benefit of stimulating conversation with your kids, you should also join them in staying well informed on the trends that fuel and even spin off from the world of hip-hop.

What better way to do this than by sharing a subscription to today's colorful and, yes, quality hip-hop magazines. These will keep your child interested because of the slammin' pictures (I personally like those "conservative" bathing suit pictures of Mary J. Blige and Foxy Brown—a totally professional attitude, you see), punchy slang, and, of course, the popularity of the artists they write about. The articles often can be controversial, political, and savvy. Recently, *Source* magazine guest journalist, the esteemed poet Sonia Sanchez, penned an article on Alfeni Shakur, mother of the deceased 2Pac and former Black Panther Party member, discussing 2Pac's life and times and his impact on the culture. Another article provided ten easy steps to eliminating meat from our diets. *Vibe* magazine had a fascinating story on Congressman J. C. Watts Jr., an Oklahoma Republican, whom they referred to as Black Caesar because of his political power and assertive style. Now, do you think you could ever get your kids to read this kind of stuff in *U.S. News and World Report?* Word!

Finally, the Answer!

So, finally, what's the answer to the original question: Is hip-hop music and culture good or bad for our kids?

That depends on many factors, some of which we have control over, some we don't. If you have little effective discipline over your child, if the child is experiencing emotional or behavioral problems or experimenting with drugs, then hip-hop can have a more negative impact. This is especially true if hip-hop is the major influence in your child's life.

A troubled child can easily identify with and be encouraged by the antisocial behavior reflected in some of the music and videos. He will see gangsta images as reinforcement of his negative behaviors. Hip-hop will become his friend and offer solace because it often reflects the anger, anxiety, and hopelessness of being black and broke. The troubled teen will embrace it as part of or addition to his antisocial or menacing image. Misery loves company.

On the other hand, if you have a teenager whose interests are well-balanced, is academically strong, has a network of positive friends, and has goals and ambitions, then you have little to worry about. A well-rounded child has likely developed enough judgment and confidence to accept hip-hop's positive values and reject the negative values it communicates.

Whether the child is troubled or stable, the relationship the two of you develop as parent and child and the support you offer will go a long way toward the development of a child who can cope and succeed in today's society, despite the negative influences of hip-hop.

A Message for Parents Who Don't Like Hip-hop

Another very important point to keep in mind is that the attitude you, as a parent, have toward hip-hop and your child's affinity to this music can also influence how your child reacts to or embraces the values put forth by this culture. What we as parents must understand is that the youth of today have rallied to hip-hop in the same fanatical way that we in our generation enjoyed blues, rock 'n' roll, jazz, R&B, and soul. These genres were filled with associations of sex and drugs, and despite the ravings of our parents, we survived. As parents, we are regrettably older but hopefully wiser, though we still haven't learned from our parents' mistaken beliefs. Like them, we seem to fear and hold preconceived notions about our children and the power of the music over their lives. Doesn't it sometimes feel that the more we try to pull them from the music, the more we end up pushing them toward it?

This phobia about hip-hop has created a real generation and communication gap with our children. The bottom line is that we must confront and resolve this fear in order to get closer to our kids. As a parent, I lost my fear of hip-hop when I watched the menacing Coolio play a genie on the television sitcom *Sabrina: The Teenage Witch*. Busta Rhymes, the hyperkinetic rapper, has been a guest star on *Cosby*. LL Cool J has his own hit comedy TV show, *In the House,* and *Men in Black*'s Will Smith is one of today's most popular Hollywood stars among both blacks and whites and was voted by *People* magazine one of the most powerful men in Hollywood. Puff Daddy had film director Penny Marshall doing his birthday announcements. Master P. was written up in *Newsweek* as being an astute businessman.

What is all this telling us? That hip-hop culture is today's culture, and we all share in it to some degree. So you can see, we really have nothing to fear. If we can learn to better understand and respect this musical genre and our children's identification with it, it will be easier to understand, respect, and talk to our children. We can get them to take hip-hop for what it's worth and think more critically about the values it imparts.

The Buck Stops With Our Kids

Finally, it all comes down to our children and the choices they make in life. That's where the parenting buck stops. We can try to guide, mentor, and even command as much as possible, but we can't always be there when our children are faced with the decisions of life, whether it's during a moment of passion and making the responsible decision about sex, or being offered a joint at a party where everyone else is smoking. These are the times where our kids must count on their own ethics, moral teachings, and judgment, learned not just from hip-hop, but more importantly from their upbringing. From *you*.

MC Maurice, a young Haitian-American brother and aspiring hip-hop and rap artist, visited my office a short while ago after I invited him for a talk about hip-hop. We kicked it on a couple of topics. He agreed that hip-hop has an extremely powerful pull on generations X, Y, and Z. He also felt that, positive or negative, hip-hop has a truthful message, one that communicates the emotional struggles of kids today—the struggle to do the right thing—and despite the influences of the street culture, a struggle to make the right choices. MC Maurice captured this sentiment in a hip-hop piece he wrote for this book:

Positive and Negative

From society, why not a day, without a night,
Bloodshed cause the life to become dead.
If it's thugs then it's crime mixed with drugs.
However you take it, if you don't like it,
Find a way to change it or escape it.

Life is what you make it,
If you have an option that fits you take it.
NEGATIVE OR POSITIVE,
It's how you live, what you receive,
Plus what you give to be an individual,
It's all in your head like it's psychological.
Mind, minded thoughts, the right choices.

And, yes, Maurice does talk to his parents!

11

Hell! Hell! The Gang's All Here!

Things are really getting bad for kids out there. They are getting slashed left and right. They are being beaten up. And a lot of this living hell is happening right in the schools.

What is causing a lot of this violence? Gangs! There is a new proliferation of gang activity among black youth, both boys and girls. There are many gangs in existence, such as the Latin Kings, the Black Gangster Disciple Nation, and the Vice Lords, but the two biggest and notorious gangs out there now are the Bloods and the Crips. These two gangs, which originated in California prisons and have become legends on the streets of Los Angeles, have now spread east and are present on the streets of major cities around the country. These gangs are also well represented in prisons all around the country.

The influence of these two gangs, and gangs in general, has been devastating to the lives of young black kids. They have been able to get members not just among poor kids but have also inserted themselves into the lives of middle-class black children who are suffering the angst of their teenage years. Inner-city black children in major cities such as New York, Los Angeles, and Boston are joining or being forcibly recruited into these two gangs in record numbers. At least four hundred thousand youths are estimated to be in gangs nationwide.

Violent street gangs are active in almost all medium- and large-size cities in America.

"I tried my best, but I don't know how much I can take," proclaimed Holly Charles, thirty-four, after her sixteen-year-old son Dwayne Johnson, a Crips member, was found guilty in August 1998 of attempting to murder an eighteen-year-old boy from a rival gang by slamming his head with a hammer and cutting his face with a cleaver. Johnson will spend the next five years in a Boston-area youth detention facility. The victim still has a prominent scar and nightly headaches to remind him that gang membership is a losing proposition.

Teen rebellion is a time of estrangement from parents, and since gangs appeal to kids who need a "family,' these kids are vulnerable to aspects of gang membership. Middle-class parents, who don't think it can happen to their children, are usually caught by surprise when they discover that their children have joined a gang.

Children as young as nine and ten years old are being lured into these gangs while attending school. It is not uncommon for gang activity to be part of daily school life. As a matter fact, this is where most of the recruitment takes place. This is a major reason why many schools have such problems with kids carrying makeshift weapons such as razor blades and box cutters. The kids claim they need these weapons for protection against gang members (who carry deadlier weapons, such a guns) trying to force them to join. Without a doubt, one of the major causes of violence in public schools is the presence of gangs.

Even good kids who avoid gangs can get into trouble. Bianca, a pretty fifteen-year-old, was brought to my clinic suffering from post-traumatic stress disorder caused by her being slashed across the face in school and left with a prominent scar (a fate worse than death for a fifteen-year-old girl). It seems that three girls from a local gang offered her membership, she refused, and was sliced as a message to other potentially resistant girls.

Why Gang Membership?

Why is gang membership attractive? Why has membership increased? Why have young blacks been especially drawn to gang life? There are a number of reasons:

Low Self-Esteem

As always, children with low self-esteem are at risk for antisocial and aberrant behavior because they try to compensate and falsely build up esteem, often by breaking the rules of acceptable behavior. It is also easier for the child with low self-esteem to fall into the wrong crowd, such as a gang, because membership brings emotional and physical security. Even thinking is made easier because of the gang's group mentality.

The Lure of Money and Status

Gangs are admired and feared, whether you want to join them or not. They are seen as the top dogs on the street and in the schools. They rule by numbers, fear, and intimidation. They set fashion trends and inspire movies, music, and clothing. In many ways, they are the new mafia, exhibiting women, wealth, and power. Black kids tend to see gang leaders as success stories and can't relate to the real successes of the black community— the working dads and moms, the local shop owners, and even the mailman who delivers the mail every day and makes an honest, clean living.

Poverty

Being poor, of course, puts black youth at risk for a multitude of academic, behavioral, and emotional problems. Being poor creates a feeling of malaise, a sense of powerlessness, and feelings of anger. To a teen who feels disenfranchised and discarded by society, gang membership channels all these feelings and offer a sense of importance and belonging. Instead of being ignored, the new gang member is now feared and, in some perverse way, admired. "Gang-banging" (hanging out, beating up rival members) becomes, in effect, recreation and a misguided way to release energy.

Drug Trade

The major business of gangs is the drug trade and, with the prevalence of crack cocaine, it has become a very big business indeed. Many senior gang members regard recruitment of young people as a way to get new and energetic labor for their drug-selling businesses. These kids make more money in one day selling drugs than some adults make in a week of honest work. Other lesser-known gangs have become more powerful and dangerous than Mafia crime families by having so many kids selling drugs in their own neighborhoods. Kids are recruited because, if and when they get arrested, their juvenile status enables them to avoid jail sentences, or serve only minimal time, and get back on the streets quickly.

Prisons and Jails

A surprising number of young blacks (and Latinos) populate our jails and prisons, where the drug culture is firmly entrenched. Right now over one million black males are currently incarcerated, according to U.S. Department of Justice statistics, with another 978,000 black men on probation. At New York City's Rikers Island facility, for example, the vast majority of inmates are black and Latino.

The Bloods, Crips, and Latin Kings, as well as dozens of other gangs, immediately confront new inmates upon their arrival. Often these neophytes have no choice but to join these gangs for protection to avoid being robbed, beaten, and raped. However, membership is not revoked upon release from jail, so gang affiliation is carried to the streets, where members continue to recruit.

Teen Rebellion

Gang life has encouraged, supported, and even required acting-out behaviors such as stealing cars, drive-by shootings, and selling drugs. In a two-state study of gang activity in Colorado and Florida, 93.6 percent gang members reported stealing a car, 72.3 percent reported selling drugs, and 64.2 percent reported committing a homicide. Kids who never had behavioral or academic problems are now embracing gang membership as a rite of passage. I have talked to many kids who feel that it's what you're supposed to do in order to prove that you're hip or cool.

Marcel, a first generation Haitian-American, was brought to my clinic for therapy because of his bad attitude and defiant behavior. His parents, who raised him in a strict Caribbean manner, witnessed his steady decline from being a conscientious and kind honor student to becoming a common thug. His grades dropped rapidly. After some of his friends joined a gang out of boredom, Marcel went with the crowd and joined too. He was ripe for the group because he saw that as a way to provide independence and rebel against his rigid upbringing. Marcel felt he was doing nothing wrong and was very proud of his new friends, who happened to be his fellow Blood members. Marcel eventually dropped out of group therapy and continued to defy his parents, who felt powerless, and shortly thereafter he was arrested and jailed at Rikers Island for the possession of a loaded gun.

Family Matters

It is common knowledge that one of the most typical reasons people join gangs is to get the family life they did not get at home. I cannot repeat enough that good family life is the key to keeping your children away from bad influences and ensuring that they thrive. Familial bonds are the most important weapons against rebellious behaviors. When these are missing, gang life becomes the major option. As proof of this, many kids, especially girls who come from sexually and or physically abusive homes, cherish gang membership as offering the love and support they never received.

So strong is this sense of family in gang membership that many members stay in the gangs even after becoming adults, holding jobs, and raising families. In a New York public school, a teacher was relieved of his duties when it was discovered that he was still an active member of the Latin Kings! New York broadcaster and social activist Felipe Luciano, a former gang member, often lectures about the false and often fatal attractions of gang membership. It was his love of his real biological family and his personal ambition that motivated him to escape gang life. Luciano is living proof that gang members can be successfully converted into good citizens, and you can see him on local New York television on Sunday mornings.

Violence 'R' Us

Gangs have always had a reputation for being violent, but today's gangs are especially vicious. During the past fifteen years, eighty-three gang leaders accumulated 834 arrests, 37 percent for violent crimes ranging from domestic violence to murder. A major reason for this is the long-standing feud between the Crips, Bloods, Latin Kings, and others to protect turf, as well as expand and maintain drug operations. And we're not talking about *West Side Story* rumbles anymore. Unlike the gangs of yesteryear, who duked it out with fists, bats, and occasional knives, today's gangs use military-style firepower.

Violence is part of the basic fabric of these groups. Incredibly about 90 percent of gang members carry concealed weapons, according to a recent study. Initiations sometimes involve mutilations of the skin to display the markings of the gangs. It doesn't end there. In order to resign membership in some of the tougher gangs, the exiting member must endure a savage beating. These are only some of the reasons gang membership is hazardous to your child's health and must be avoided at all costs!

Signs of Gang Activity

A major problem for parents in addressing this issue is that they do not know how susceptible their kids are to membership in a gang or if, in fact, they already are active in one. The following are some of the signs of interest or actual gang membership.

Colors and Clothes Make the Man!

Bloods have chosen red as their symbol (you mess with them and you bleed red), while the Crips have taken on blue (cross them and they will beat you black and blue). Gang members are required to wear their colors in either the form of a shirt, coat, or kerchief worn on the head or sticking out the back pocket. As a form of insanity, gang members will attack other kids who are not gang members but are wearing these colors. Some school-children refuse to wear red or blue for fear of being attacked. So if you start noticing your child wearing one of these colors consistently, there may be something going on.

Clothing signals among gangs include: wearing caps tilted to one side or the other, earrings in left or right ear, and wearing the belt buckle to one side.

Winston, a skinny sixteen-year-old, was brought to group sessions at my clinic by his mother, who suspected that he was in a gang or about to join one, which he denied. However, he started wearing blue as a primary dress color. When his mother brought him a bright red shirt for Christmas, he refused to wear it. He was already in the Crips, and blue is their compulsory color!

Branding

Initiation into the gang includes being marked with the name of the gang, usually carved into the shoulder with a sharp knife. This marking, or tattoo, is known as a badge. They can also look like distinctive designer logos. And, of course, the Bloods' tattoo is in red; the Crips' is in blue.

Unfriendly Friends

Out of nowhere, your child may have acquired new friends who will stick very close to him. They will usually attend school together, travel together, and hang out together; all the time. Typically, gang members are not friendly with parents and other adults, and will keep their distance. If your kid's friends do no speak with you or you just can't seem to get a handle on who they really are, then there is a something to hide and I think we know that it is.

A teen that I was counseling would come to group sessions with a pack of three or four friends. His gang comrades would actually stay in the waiting room while he was in the session! It almost seemed as if they were babysitting him. I later overheard them grilling him to make sure he didn't mention their gang.

Secrecy

Loyalty and silence are a basic part of membership in a gang. Therefore, your child will probably communicate with you much less. He may become cagey or secretive when questioned about his activities. He will likely withdraw from family involvement, stay out late, and break rules.

Defiance

If your child begins to become extraordinarily belligerent and resistant to all authority, gang membership may be behind the bravado. If your child is not afraid to take you on, he is probably answering to the gang as his authority.

Imitation of Gang Life

The kid will have gangsta-influenced music, usually gangsta rap, videos, books, and movies. In imitation of the gangsta lifestyle, he will also wear a lot of jewelry and medallions.

Drug and Alcohol Use

With gang membership comes an increase in drug and alcohol use—malt liquor, beer, marijuana, and "blow" (cocaine). Part of the gangsta mentality is to hang out, get high, and get into trouble. A little "jump-start" always helps.

Other Signs

Other signs of possible gang membership include: the sudden appearance of gang symbols or graffiti on notebooks, homework, and in lockers, and an abrupt drop in school grades with an increase in tardiness and absences. Carrying a pager or beeper was originally a bad sign, but today it is no cause for alarm unless other signs are present.

Rescuing Kids From Gangs

If your worst fears are confirmed and your child is actually in a gang, there is only one thing that you can do, and that's to get him out of its clutches as quickly as possible. Delaying even one day can mean the difference between life and death. I know it's scary and it's going to be tough, but there are some effective strategies that will help you to save your child.

Discuss your concerns with your child. Discuss how much you love him and how you are concerned about his safety. Talking about love doesn't come easy to many people, but desperate times require desperate measures. If he is estranged, bring him back into the fold. However, if he is not willing to listen, especially if you are asking him to leave the gang, you may have to snatch him out and heavily monitor his behavior. And you may need to call on the community relations department of your local police precinct.

Keep tabs on your child at all times. Gang members like to travel in small groups. If fellow gang members are shadowing your child constantly you may want to mimic this behavior, accompanying your child wherever he or she goes when not in school. Of course, this will require a tremendous amount of time, but it will be worth it.

The court system can help. If your child is in a gang and is out of control, you may need the assistance of family court. This system has social workers, probation, parole, and community relations personnel who can monitor your child's whereabouts and provide you with resources, such as counseling and conflict resolution, to address the negative behaviors. Some court programs will actually send an expert, usually a former gang member who has expertise in negotiating the release of a child from gang membership, if you are unable to handle it on your own.

You may want to play hard ball and make sure that any illegal activity committed by your child and his friends is reported to the police. Of course, this is tough love (a mixture of toughness and warmth) to the extreme, but sometimes you have to draw the line and let your child suffer the consequences and learn a lesson the hard way, even if it means jail time or, at least, the threat of it.

Send your child away to live with out-of-state relatives or to a disciplinary or boarding school. Fabled musician Louis Armstrong was sent to a reform school, where he learned to play the trumpet. Actor Steve McQueen got straightened out at a reform school in Chino, California. And Brooklyn-born champ Mike Tyson, after getting out of reform school, lived with trainer Cus D'Amato and his wife in the Catskills while honing his boxing skills.

Get him to join the armed forces if all else fails. The services have straightened out many rebellious young men. Believe it or not, teens beg for rules and structure. Don't be too afraid of his fighting a war on foreign soil, as he is already fighting one on the city streets as part of the gang. He may really go for the security and regimentation of service life. Stop by a recruiting office and pick up some of their persuasive literature. At worst, your son will learn a trade. In a better case scenario, he will get a college education, courtesy of Uncle Sam, and a career.

Call in the police, if necessary, to help protect your child from what I call the gang exit interview: a severe beating. If you are able to get your child out of the gang, he may be hunted down to receive this punishment. Believe me, you don't want this to happen. Some kids don't survive it. The presence of the police may be helpful, but not foolproof. If nothing else, the gang members will know that you are serious about getting your child back, and like the robber who bypasses houses protected by alarm systems, they may not want to be bothered with you.

Charlene was being shadowed and taunted by the female gang she belonged to after her mother convinced her to leave. They consistently threatened her with the horror and humiliation of the exit beating, which scared and intimidated her. Charlene's boyfriend solved the problem by calling the police every time the girls threatened. The gang became so frustrated and hassled that after a few weeks they finally gave up. Charlene got away without the beating, and she and her mother now help other girls in the same situation.

Keep Them Out Before They Go In

I cannot stress enough that prevention is always the best treatment. And, of course, there are ways of keeping your kids from joining gangs or even keeping informal company with them.

Keep the lines of communication open with your kids:
This is the most important thing that you can do. Not only do you establish a trusting relationship with your children, you'll also be knowledgeable about what goes on in their lives. If they are being approached by or even gravitating toward a gang, you'll know about it and can take immediate steps.

Good communication with your children will also allow you to be open to their needs. You will know how to keep a sense of family and provide the emotional fuel that offers that ever important sense of belonging and support. These are the same values that the gangs provide, so beat them to it.

Keep your kids constantly busy:
Have them attend after-school programs, music lessons, or team sports. If they are doing something with clear goals and

ambitions, they won't have time to indulge in negativity. Accompany them to their activities; take to shows and plays; just keep them busy and stimulated.

Don't ever lose parental control:

Discipline is the key—don't let kids cross the line or intimidate you. They need rules, so make sure you provide them and enforce them:

- Do not allow body markings. If your child has gang-related tattoos, go to a dermatologist and have them removed.
- If they violate the curfew, immediately punish them by taking away a privilege.
- If you see gang marking on their books, have them erased or crossed out.
- Stop giving out an allowance or spending money if you know it is being spent on gang or drug paraphernalia.

The bottom line—take charge. Children are like sheep—they need a strong herder to lead them. We, as parents, go wrong when we start to allow backsliding by our kids. When we let a situation get out of control without action, the next thing you know a pattern of antisocial behavior has developed. If your competitor is the gang, you will need to be strong in raising your child. If you cannot be a parental leader, I'm sure the gang leader will be more than happy to step in and take your place.

Join and encourage community programs:

You can help improve your child's self-esteem, sense of purpose, (and those of others) by actively participating in community affairs. Help develop and maintain programs involving crime prevention, neighborhood watches, drug abuse, child abuse, and job training. Ensure that the local police precinct is involved and keep them informed of relevant activities. Gangs simply do not thrive in neighborhoods with strong community programs.

One tip: If you can't contribute your time to any community programs, make a point of meeting the people in your neighborhood who are active and pass along your ideas and suggestions. Activists appreciate the input and it helps them formulate community priorities.

Fight the Power:

Gangs have tremendous status, influence, and power, all of

which impresses impressionable kids, especially those with low self-esteem. Therefore, expose your kids to more productive role models to show them how money and power can also come from hard work. Take them to visit black professionals at law firms, medical clinics, or large corporations.

In addition, try to keep them in nice clothes and encourage good dressing and grooming so they look like winners. Encourage them to develop a style that they feel is their own, as opposed to a gang uniform.

Take Your children to church:

One of the major things missing in many families today, the glue that holds people together, is a sense of spirituality. I believe that spirituality plays a very important part in a family's strength and a child's positive development. It is my unscientific opinion that children who have been raised with God in their hearts and in their thoughts turn out to be emotionally stronger human beings when they grow up. These are the kids who have the intestinal fortitude to resist many of life's temptations, especially the lure and excitement of the gang.

Your child does not necessarily have to become a pew-shaking, Bible-thumping religious fanatic (though that's okay, too). The idea is to foster a belief in some kind of higher power— a good, positive force that will keep him spiritually strong to resist the gang. Involvement in church activities, including outings, also leads to meeting other good people and keeps your child busy.

Tyrell, a stocky fifteen-year old, was getting involved in gang activity on its fringes. His mother sensed trouble, took him to church, and signed hum up for Sunday school, Bible study, and the choir. Tyrell did not like going to church at first, but his mother insisted, and also made sure the younger deacon (who had also been "wild" once) talked to him about his experiences and how he turned around. She bought him an easy-reading Bible to thumb through, and he became interested enough to learn the Ten Commandments by memory. He also liked reading proverbs, which were short and understandable. The choirmaster, sensing Tyrell's talent, soon trained him to become a featured soloist. Now fully involved in church, he is learning to play the piano organ. Rumor has it that he also found a female friend in the girls' choir.

Your Efforts Will Be Rewarded

In the short run, your children may be resentful over your meddling in their lives, feel restricted, and even get really angry with you. But trust me on this one—they'll get over it. And when they become successful and raise their own children, they will always remember you for your love and heroism in keeping them away or rescuing them from one of the most destructive influences they'll ever have faced.

12

MULTIRACIAL CHILDREN: IT'S NOT JUST BLACK OR WHITE ANYMORE

> If you're white you're right,
> If you're black stay back
> If you're *brown* stick around.

WHETHER IT WAS HANNIBAL who conquered the lands and women of Sicily or the systematic rape of slave women by their white masters in the New World, race mixing has always been a part of human history. In the United States alone there are two million mixed marriages and one and a half million mixed-race children.

Being part of an interracial relationship or marriage can be a very trying experience, especially since many people are uncomfortable with the mixing of the races. As bad as it is for parents in interracial relationships, it's even worse for their children. And let's not forget lighter-skinned black children who carry some Caucasian blood because of a distant relative; these children also suffer. Black children who have nontraditional physical attributes, are typically viewed by blacks and whites as being neither black nor white, or by blacks as not being black enough and by whites as not being white enough.

Children of mixed race are emotionally and socially affected in many ways. If their parents are shunned for engaging in an interracial relationship, then most likely their mixed-race children will encounter the same hostile or ambivalent treatment. They may also feel disliked or envied, especially by their black peers, because of their nontraditional physical attributes. Because the children of most interracial unions receive characteristics of both races, their skin color is most often lighter; their hair is usually finer—sometimes combined with straight and kinky tresses; and their eye color is mostly of a lighter hue than what a typical black person might possess. Also, the size and shape of the nose might be narrower, and their lips may not appear as full. Therefore, it becomes very easy for this type of a child to have problems developing a racial identity. Quite often, especially in the younger years, this is extremely difficult. And even if they do develop one they may still be shunned by the members of that particular racial group, resulting in a profound sense of rejection.

Carla, a patient of biracial heritage, tearfully described in therapy how her white mother was never offered any support from her mother (Carla's maternal grandmother), who refused to accept the fact that her daughter had married a black man. Due to the manifestation of intergenerational prejudice, Carla's grandmother also wanted no relationship with Carla or her siblings, who loved and identified with their white mother. This rejection resulted in Carla accepting a black identity, almost by default. But to add insult to injury, this rejection was repeated again during her college years. Carla was considered attractive by most of the students. She was of light complexion, with long curly hair and gray eyes. The guys always wanted to be in her company, For this reason, many black females on campus disliked Carla or were jealous of what they thought was her exotic beauty. She was ostracized by the female students who thought she perceived herself as being better than the other girls. This is what drove Carla to therapy: She had been rejected by her grandmother for being part black and had been later rejected by her fellow black students for being part white! The result was depression and a lifetime of self-depreciation.

Caste, Class, and Their Effect
on Mixed-Race Children

Much of the confusion and prejudice surrounding mixed-race children comes from the class and caste system in black society, in which mixed or light-skinned blacks are considered "better," to a certain point, than darker blacks. Historically, blacks have had a love-hate relationship with the different shades of black skin and features. This color divide has been going on since the days of slavery. Back then, darker-skinned slaves were consigned to the fields and in the kitchens, while the lighter and "less-offensive" looking slaves were for the most part, allowed the "privilege" of becoming the more prestigious house slaves. The house slaves were allowed to travel with their masters and were even allowed to read and write, and in many cases bore the babies of their white masters. (This fact has resurfaced in earnest with the discovery of DNA evidence showing that Sally Hemmings, the mulatto slave of Thomas Jefferson, may have born at least one of his children.) Though the light-skinned blacks were the elite slaves, admired by less fortunate, darker slaves for the "whiter" appearance, there was also jealousy and dislike for their good fortune.

This scenario has been carried down through the years and adversely and obscenely affected black culture. A prime example of this occurred during the early 1900s, when the elite, historically black colleges and universities were flourishing in the South. Many required prospective students to submit photographs with their applications for admission. Unbe-knownst to qualifying students, this was a part of the school's elimination process. Some colleges did not admit students not because of mediocre academic performance, but because they had too much melanin in their skin—they were too dark. More light-skinned blacks were usually admitted into these colleges. Light, bright, damned near white was a slogan that described most of the female coeds. It is surprising to visit these schools during reunion time and see dozens of older graduates who appear white in every way, but they are black. At Howard University, the school of choice for upper-middle-class blacks in the 1950s, if the color of your skin was darker than a brown paper bag you were not allowed to hang out or associate with the "elite" light-skinned blacks! Because of this behavior, all light-skinned blacks at the school were often disliked because they were perceived as carrying themselves as "high yellow niggas." Of course, this would be very unfair and cause hardship and a rejection of racial identification for those light-skinned or mixed blacks who completely identified with being Afrocentric.

With this kind of legacy, is it any wonder that black children of mixed race or light skinned black children are in conflict and confused about their heritage and racial identity? Not only is it difficult for them to establish a black identity because of their outward appearance, it becomes even tougher when they are not accepted by their fellow blacks! As much as they are accorded a certain status because of their lineage, they are, at the same time, put down because of it. The term "tragic mulatto" has evolved from the lives of mixed-race or light-skinned blacks who were accorded a certain privilege by whites and blacks but not accepted by either as an equal member.

Patricia, age forty-five, who I counseled in therapy for many years, was born from black parents where there had been some race mixing from a few generations back. Consequently, she was born with light eyes, hair, and skin. From as far back as she could remember, her experiences with other blacks were bittersweet. Though they admired her for being light, at the same time, she was put down for it, often being referred to as "high yellow." Her experiences with whites were much more pleasant. For the whites who thought that she was white, she was accorded privileges usually reserved for Caucasians. Though she was not ashamed of being a black person, she slowly became accustomed to this preferential treatment. By the time she went to high school, her status of being treated as if she were "white," allowed her to avoid the prejudices and discrimination aimed at darker skinned blacks. In college she grew tired of being pursued by black male students because of her light skin and being scorned by the black female students for the same attribute. Upon graduating college, she made the decision to pass for white. To carry this off meant severing previous friendships. And though her parents suspected what she was doing, they never confronted her, which she interpreted as a lack of emotional support. Eventually, there was an emotional toll to be paid. Patricia began to develop a severe depression and growing lack of self-respect, simply because she was not being true to herself. Therapy helped her come to terms with her emotional conflicts, but she suffered long and hard before she sought treatment. I often wonder how many other light-skinned black children or black children of mixed race are following in Patricia's footsteps and will suffer through because of these issues?

As is therefore evident, black children of mixed race and/or of lighter skin, must deal with many social issues and are usually left carrying a lot of emotional baggage. Having the status of being an "other" has caused these children to have emotional and maturational problems that if not addressed can lead to a lifetime of difficulties, including behavioral problems, academic difficulties, and poor interpersonal relationships. After all, if you are uncomfortable with yourself, or don't know who you are, how can you gain the confidence to successfully interact with others?

A Lack of Black Identity

To further elucidate this problem, in our often racist society it is tough enough for a black child to establish a racial identity, especially a black one. It becomes even tougher when they are labeled and treated as being "other." I have counseled many mixed-race children who are caught in the dilemma of not knowing who or what they are.

Vincent, whose mother is white and whose father is black, was brought in for therapy because he was getting more and more depressed as well as failing in school. After some time together, we got down to the root of the problem. Vincent looked almost completely white and not black. His friends and girlfriend were all white. The big problem was that Vincent looked white, talked white, walked white, and thought white. However, he began to experience feelings about being black. At the same time, his confusion worsened because he often overheard friends making disparaging statements about blacks. His father, whom he had viewed as being colorless, he now saw as black, which awakened many questions for him: Am I black, white, or something in between? Since race was rarely discussed at home, Vincent did not think that he could share his feelings with anyone, especially his parents. As a result, he became angry and depressed.

Color Me Denial

As a result of this identity or color crisis, many children of mixed race often go through a "denial" phase in which they view themselves as being neither black nor white, but a separate race called mixed. It is the rare, very mature child who can transcend race and view himself as a separate entity, neither black nor white but "other." Most children who classify themselves as "other" mistakenly believe, consciously or unconsciously, that this status excludes them from having to experience the trials and tribulations of being black. For some kids, this phase may be more intense than others. Around this time last year I was a guest expert on *The Maury Povich Show* along with several young people of color who were of mixed race. They had started a political movement to be able to have a new racial category called mixed race. They intelligently spoke of being neither black nor white, but a hybrid of both. And even though they gave excellent presentations, I could not help but shake my head with sorrow at the apparent confusion and conflict these children were experiencing in denying their blackness.

How to Keep Your Mixed Kids From Becoming Mixed Up

Once again, it comes back to you as parents and what you can do through smart parenting to help your mixed-race children understand and accept who and what they are in order to lead emotionally healthy and productive lives. What follows are some strategies that have proven to be effective for many of the parents and children with whom I have worked around these issues.

- Before your child can understand and accept a physical and/or emotional mixed-race inheritance, she must learn to understand and accept the status and significance of being first and foremost black. In other words, it is important that she develop a black racial identity. No matter how small her nose, no matter how thin her lips, no matter how straight her hair; she is first and foremost *black* and should be proud. Why black first? The answer is simple. Being black is the hardest thing in the world, bar none. It truly does take a lifetime to come to terms with being perceived and treated as an inferior being, no matter your education, no matter your accomplishments. It is impossible for a child to appreciate other contributing cultures and blood-lines if she cannot first accept the true basis of her nature and racial identity. You can help your child accomplish this ever important maturational step by surrounding her with the beauty of Africa, the Caribbean, and black America. This can be done through family photographs, music, and magazines such as *Essence, Ebony,* and *Unfold,* which most often feature dark-skinned models. In 1998 there was a major flap over a white New York public school teacher's classroom use of a book entitled *Nappy Hair,* by Carolivia Herron (an African-American scholar), to teach diversity to her third-grade class. The book depicts a black girl's eventual acceptance of and pride in her coarse and unruly head of hair. Though there have also been many objections by black parents to the term *nappy hair,* this book, as well as others, can help our black children, especially those of mixed race, to accept and embrace their African culture, characteristics, and features with pride.

- During the early years of development, a child's belief and ideas are a direct result of what their parents think and do. If you are a mixed-race parent or are a partner in an inter-racial relationship, openly address your multiculturalism— the positives *and* the negatives. Too many parents in this situation ignore race as a factor that will affect all family members to a different degree. Once Vincent's parents openly discussed the issue of mixed race in family discus-sions, it allowed him the opportunity to appropriately address his difficulties from being of mixed race and establish a distinct identity.

- It also goes without saying that if you are a mixed-race parent or are light-skinned and do not openly acknowledge your blackness, chances are your child will not either.

Verbalize your pride in being both mixed *and* black. This will set an example that in turn will help your child accept her unique racial makeup and blackness.

During a group therapy discussion on childhood, Kelli, a group patient, described growing up half Irish and black. Though she was confident in her mixed-race heritage and saw herself as being black, she never felt she had to justify it to anyone. However, when she gave birth to her mixed-race son (his father was full black Jamaican), she noticed that he had many questions about his heritage and some confusion about his racial identity, since he had a few bloodlines. It was at that point that she began to verbalize her pride in being part Irish but also her firm conviction and identification with being a black person. Her actions and behavior quickly erased any confusion he had about his identity, and though he definitely looks mixed, he squarely identifies himself as being a black child of mixed blood.

- Once you have assisted your child in affirming pride in her African heritage, then you can and should begin the next step of introducing pictures, music, photographs, and children's books that reflect the diverse races and bloodlines in the family. Integrating the purely African with the mixed-race images will allow your child to begin to develop a *balanced* sense of self. As part of this effort, educate your child to the fact that black people come in all sizes, shapes *and colors*. Use examples of relatives, friends, and even celebrities to bring the point home. For example, the teen idol Brandy, comedian Jamie Foxx, and the Wayans brothers are dark, while Mariah Carey, actress Halle Berry, and singer Vanessa Williams are mixed race and light in appearance, but they are all black people! This will begin to clarify to your child the multiculturalism that is part of being black. This is extremely important during the early years, especially infancy, when babies see different colors and sometimes display certain moods associated with color.

Melissa is Mexican and her husband, Travis, is an extremely light-skinned black. Most of their family members are mixed and lighter skinned. They have a seven-year-old daughter, Normandi, who is now very much accepting of the different shades of black, but they had to work at getting her to that point. At age one or two she would scream and cry whenever approached by darker-skinned people. She was never exposed to them, and became fearful of this different color. As her parents consciously exposed her to darker people, she became more comfortable. They also started buying her multiracial children's books and black dolls. Without this effort to teach her about the different shades and mixtures of black people, she may have developed a distrust of darker-skinned people and not have accepted her black heritage.

- Allow your child to explore feelings and questions about their color or race in a nonthreatening environment. For example, when my daughter asks what color she is, I tell her she is black. Quite often she will respond, "no daddy, I'm white." I don't give her a hard time, or tell her that she is wrong, for that would only add to her confusion and anxiety. Instead, I respond, "It's true, the color of your skin is white, but your soul, your heritage, and who you are is black. Your mommy and daddy are also black, but just like you we have different skin colors, like brown and yellow." I have created an environment where we can revisit this issue as often as she wants.

- Don't give mixed messages to your child, one minute praising her because of an exotic appearance, encouraging feelings of superiority, and then later scolding her for thinking she is better than her friends and relatives who are darker or not of mixed race. This will result in a very confused child who will be lost when it comes to developing feelings of self-worth, especially regarding her racial identity. A good way to avoid this problem entirely is to give positive messages that do not emphasize mixed-race attributes.

One of my young Hispanic patients, Davina, who is lighter than any of her immediate family, was often told by her mother, in front of her sisters, that she looked like the "child of rich people." The feelings of superiority she developed because of such statements caused her severe problems fitting in with her sisters, as well as jealousy between them. In family therapy, the first thing I did was to point out that the messages expressed by her parents encouraged Davina to feel superior, but also caused her conflict in the family. I urged the parents to focus instead on providing messages that were positive but not based on the physical attributes of a particular race. Here are some examples:

No: "Your hair is so pretty and *fine*," or "You have *good* hair."

Yes: "Your hair is pretty."

No: "Your lips are so *thin* and attractive."

Yes: "Your mouth is attractive."

No: "Your skin color is so light, you can pass for white."

Yes: "Your skin is very nice."

The new messages helped her build and maintain self-worth, but at the same time did not segregate or place her apart from her siblings because of her looks.

Finally, as with any kind of parenting, always keep open communication with your child, and help guide him through the confusion of being of mixed race with sympathy, dignity and consistency. He will need your guidance and strength especially because the maturational issues of black children of mixed race have not yet been defined as an urgent national problem, nor are they part of the public consciousness. So, for the most part, other than a few programs such as the Children of the Rainbow curriculum in the public schools, help must come from home. It must come from parents.

There are still a whole lot of people out there, black and white, who still have screwed up and backward notions about mixed race, which is yet another pressure and prejudice on you black child. Smart parenting will minimize the confusion and help your child grow from this challenge.

13

Racism: A Lifelong Challenge

I HAVE SPOKEN to many white Americans, and they say, hands down, that people of all races are being treated equally, and even though racism still exists, blacks are treated equally, especially blacks living in large cities.

I have talked to blacks who feel the opposite. Ask a person of color if they are treated equally in our society, and, hands down, you will receive a resounding "Hell no!" The truth is that racism, prejudice, anti-Semitism, and sexism continue to exist in the world and, of course, in the United States. Until America confronts its prejudices head on, racism will continue.

In the meantime, black parents must prepare their children to confront and conquer prejudice so that they can pursue health, happiness, and success in their lives. However, in order to accomplish this task we must first understand the different forms of racism that exist today and their effect on our children of color.

Raw Racism

By raw racism I mean unadulterated hate and ignorance. Blacks are seen in stereotypes strictly of the most negative kind. Specifically, they are viewed as inferior and the cause of all the bad things that occur in society, especially crime. This type of thinking has historically led to blacks being beaten, maltreated, and even lynched.

Modern lynchings continue in streets all over America. In the Bensonhurst section of Brooklyn, New York, a gang of white youths beat several young blacks and killed one when the blacks crossed into the white part of town. In Rhode Island, two white off-duty cops critically injured a young black man over an unprovoked racial incident. There was no rhyme or reason for these incidents, only the pure hatred of black people, but because of these types of incidents, our young people are in danger.

Scientific Racism

This "high-tech" racism is perhaps the most insidious type. It goes back to the notion that blacks are genetically inferior. Here we find a constant push by the scientific community to connect intelligence and violence to genetics, and guess who always comes out at the bottom of this pile? The charlatan scientist William Shockley began the argument of genetic inferiority in his bogus scientific studies, but this racist banner continues to be carried by many others, including psychologists Richard J. Herrnstein and Charles Murray, authors of *The Bell Curve* (1994). They argue that funding for social programs should be cut because the social problems of blacks are caused by inferior genetics and not a racist environment.

Media Stereotypes

In my many years of working with thousands of black children, I have come to one inescapable conclusion: They have bought into the thinking that blacks are less book-smart than whites. For example, most bright black kids describe themselves as being street smart, hustlers, or wise guys, not just *smart*. They just do not believe they can achieve academically and intellectually. This lack of belief in their abilities directly affects their school performance. They are often afraid to tackle or develop an interest in subjects such as mathematics, science, or computers, which often results in their lack of preparation and eventual failure in high school and, if they get that far, college.

There are many reasons for black kids doubting their abilities or putting themselves down. I believe that the number-one reason for this defeatist thinking is the characters and role models they are fed, which are racial stereotypes.

For example, Madison Avenue and the corporate world may not be intentionally racist, but they have chosen one-dimensional black heroes purely on the basis of their athletic skills (a stereotype) to sell products. It doesn't matter that many of them don't have a college education, but if they could sell a sneaker, they'd be as good as Kool and the Gang, and that is irresponsible and racist. It perpetuates the notion to our black kids, that to be a successful black person you only have to be athletic and not intellectual. Hollywood does the same thing by portraying black characters as hustlers and thieves with hearts of gold. Sadly, our black children also accept these so-called heroes as their role models.

By the way, some of the basketball pitch men who are pushed as heroes and role models to our kids are not exactly poster boys for exemplary behavior. A recent study of NBA players under the age of thirty revealed that the average unmarried or single player had approximately five children by five different women! Not exactly the role model I would pick for my kid.

One last note here, there is a bright light, Michael Jordan. He is a pitchman for not only sports products, but also clothes, colognes, and technology. This is the type of role model Madison Avenue and Hollywood need to continue putting forward for *all* children!

Antiaffirmative Actions

Many whites and some blacks have begun dismantling affirmative action, calling it reverse discrimination. This becomes a way of saying, "You blacks have gotten enough freebies," or "Less qualified blacks are getting preferences over qualified whites!" My professional opinion is, "Bull!" These fallacies, which lead the assault on affirmative action, have directly affected the academic opportunities of black children. The chairman of the board of trustees at the University of California at Irvine, Ward Connerly (himself a black man!), recently won a public referendum to strike down affirmative action policies intended to attract talented young blacks to California colleges. The effect has been devastating, with minority enrollment down almost 90 percent from last year. Even the opponents of affirmative action believe that such drastically lower minority enrollment was too high a price to pay for the success of the referendum.

In New York City, Mayor Rudolph Giuliani and his political crony, City University of New York (CUNY) Trustee Herman Badillo, waged and won a battle against CUNY's remedial classes, which are often attended by minority students from less affluent, usually public schools. I predict that the enrollment of minority students will soon begin dropping in record numbers, devastating their opportunity for real advancement.

Institutional Racism

Racism and prejudice have been part of our society for so long that even now that the worst of it is over, the aftereffects still keep blacks down. Even though blacks are supposedly equal to whites, the reality is that whites are still on top, and for blacks to move up we have to get past the personal, and perhaps unconscious, prejudices of individual whites in all kinds of situations.

For example, in the corporate world, top managers have historically been almost exclusively white and male. Nowadays, discrimination is no longer sanctioned, and all employees—black, white, and other—are allowed to compete equally for managerial positions. However, here's where institutional racism comes in. The mostly white managers, who get to choose whom to promote, will tend to pick the "types" of people with whom they can best relate and feel "comfortable"—most likely, fellow whites. The black candidates are at a disadvantage right from the beginning.

This kind of thing happens every day, in the workplace, in schools, in social situations, and in politics. It's not necessarily hatred—it's just an aversion to someone different. Institutional racism keeps blacks from catching up to whites in terms of quality housing, career advancement, and all kinds of social and professional arenas. As long as society remains prejudiced, no matter what blacks achieve in education and status, we will still have a hard time getting through the "glass ceiling."

Take me, for example.

I have a Ph.D. in psychology, considered a high-income

profession. I have been turned down for small lines of credit, denied housing in Manhattan, and sometimes I still have trouble getting a cab because many cabbies assume that, as a black person, I don't have the wealth of a white person which translates into a smaller tip or having to drive into a "dangerous" black neighborhood. Is it any wonder that many young blacks don't buy into the notion that education guarantees success!

The Assault on the Young Black Psyche

Of course, the result of all these handicaps on the psyche of black children is, among other things, a diminished self-image and lowered self-esteem. In plain language, black children are being brainwashed into believing they are inferior to their white counterparts. Again, these ridiculous beliefs are reinforced at the earliest ages by such innocent activities as watching television, where white folks have the best jobs, best apartments, and best houses. Black folks usually live in the ghetto and speak Ebonics, and shuffle and jive!

I have seen this type of thinking in one black patient after another. In one of my therapy groups for black adolescents, it is amazing to watch as these youngsters express one negative self statement after another, such as, "I don't know if I'm going to make it through school," "I don't think I have what it takes to be successful," or "Only white kids are smart enough to go to college." Many of them have no plans for college, and their only goal is to just make it through high school. The sadder fact is that even when they do excel, opportunities and resources are being taken away. When I was a teenager, scholarships, remedial programs, and mentoring programs were abundant. Now our black kids must sometimes pass up academic opportunities because the resources of the past are no longer there. This is extremely demoralizing to our kids!

Adversity Can Breed Success

We have seen racism hurt black children in many ways, including their educational and professional opportunities.

However, in my opinion, the worst damage they can incur is the anger caused by the humiliation of a lifetime of being treated as a second-class citizen which is often internalized into self-hatred and bitterness. How many times have we seen young people lose their self-esteem and self-worth and become poisoned by the daily discrimination that they must face as part of the reality of being black. They do not believe in themselves or, worse, hate themselves. They begin to see life as a dead-end proposition, and sometimes become involved in drugs, gang activity, and other self-destructive behaviors.

However, we as parents can help our children avoid this negative path in life. We can teach them how to use racism and prejudice as fuel to prove themselves and work toward personal and professional success. We must teach them that if they do not work hard, racism will crush them. That in itself is a motivating force to do well in life!

Like the phoenix rising from the ashes, many of our black heroes were reborn from the pain of dealing with prejudice. Without this adversity, would Dr. Martin Luther King have reached the mountaintop to have a dream? Would Malcolm X have traveled the globe in search of the meaning of God and brotherhood? Would Gen. Colin Powell have struggled to become the first black five-star general of the armed forces as well as the first black man to ever be seriously considered a legitimate candidate for president of the United States, even by whites? All of these great black Americans soared to great heights because their personal mission was to succeed by smashing the barriers of racism and establish equality for themselves and for all people.

Deep down in my soul I know that my success has been fueled by my drive to overcome the odds and the stumbling blocks that have been placed in my path just because I am black. The more the doors close in my face, the harder I knock! If I didn't have to run with weights on my ankles, perhaps I would not have become such a strong emotional and spiritual warrior. The more I hear no because of my color, the more I think, "Yes, I can! Forget my color! My desire to prove the racists wrong has become a motivating force in my life!

Transforming Prejudice From Pain to Power

As a parent and a psychologist, I urge you to use smart parenting to prepare your children for the onslaught of racism and prejudice they will inevitably face as they go out into the world. Continue to teach and encourage them to always stay positive and strong in the face of adversity. In order to not crumble under the madness of racism and prejudice, they must take the high road in life. Just because they are hated, they must not hate, for this negativity is counterproductive and will stifle their intellect, spirituality, and, finally, their potential for greatness. Instead, teach your child to recycle the pain of racism into the fuel or power to achieve her potential in life. With this thought in mind, what follows are several smart parenting techniques to help your kids triumph over racism.

Don't pull any punches. Discuss with your kids the facts of life—the *real* facts of life! Discuss the long history of slavery and segregation and their lasting negative effects on both black and white people. Teach them how racism and stereotypes can adversely affect their self-perceptions and lower their self-esteem. More importantly, teach them how to overcome this problem.

For example, we discussed negative stereotypes and their effects on black children. Racial stereotypes can often be found on television. And kids easily and unconsciously incorporate these images into their thinking and self-perceptions. A good way to short-circuit this mental absorption is by spotting, questioning, and smashing these stereotypes. The Media Awareness Network has put together some excellent tips on talking to your kids about racial stereotypes:

- Look closely at the character your child sees. Voice your disapproval of stereotyped characters and explain why you disapprove. Ask your child to compare the images of race they see on television with the people they know in real life. How are they different? Are all blacks hustlers and criminals?
- Listen closely, with your child, to the voices of the bad characters in cartoons. Do they have an accent? Are the

black characters always jive talkin', Ebonics-speaking characters that I mentioned earlier?

- Deconstruct the media "reality." Talk with your kids about the people behind the programs they watch. It could be eye-opening for children to realize that TV shows, like books, are written and created by people, most of them white, with their own biases and experiences.
- Critique other media. Look at the ads for cars, clothing, and sports equipment in newspapers, magazines, and on billboards. Talk to your child about how the product is glamorized and which audiences are targeted. Who is represented in these ads as the consumer. Why are certain ethnic groups linked to certain products? Take a look at running shoe ads, for example. Why are black athletes often portrayed as "shooting hoops" and goofing around in the gym, while white athletes are shown doing serious training?
- Find programs that counter stereotypes. As much as television can stereotype people, it can also help to break down barriers. Look for shows where the cultures and talents of blacks and Hispanics are emphasized in a positive fashion, such as *Sesame Street*, the *Star Trek* series, *Reading Rainbow*, and the *Adventures of Alan Strange*.

Teach your child how to be empowered and take responsibility for his own behavior instead of attributing his failures strictly to racism. Believe me, there is nothing more psychologically damaging than blaming racism for all of life's problems or negative circumstances. A person who does this will never make it, because he is too busy complaining about how the white man has kept him down instead of doing something about it!

Richard, one of the black teens in one of my therapy groups, was born to activist parents. He grew up hearing about the evils of racism and prejudice. However, somewhere along the line something went wrong and Richard began to believe that racism was totally responsible for all of his problems. He failed most of his classes because "the teachers hate black kids." After much therapy, it became clear that Richard became a victim of his own thinking and he started using racism as a crutch. He felt he no longer had to take responsibility for his actions because everything was the white man's fault. The focus of therapy was getting him to challenge his defeatist and lazy thinking by having him challenge his perceptions as well as generate solutions to each "racial" problem he encountered. For example, if the teachers did not pass him because he was black, how did other black students manage to do well in the classes? Second, even if the teachers did not like black students, how could he still pass his classes? How could he take control? He came up with the answers:

> *Study*
> *Do homework*
> *Read*
> *Do extra assignments*
> *Work twice as hard as the white students*

By eliminating blaming behavior and instituting problem-solving thinking, Richard soon became empowered to take the responsibility of winning instead of losing, feeling sorry for himself, and blaming others. He understood that racism is part of life; it should be fought, but above all, you should never give up.

Each day, make time to sit down and review with your child the events of her day. If a racial situation presented itself, discuss how she handled it and how she might have handled it differently or better. Most importantly, help your child sort out what she has learned from the situation. This approach will quickly teach your child not to harbor bitterness but grow from the experience instead.

Do not ever let your child feel defeated by any situation especially one that is racial in nature. You can explain that racism is a daily part of a black person's life. Therefore, she must deal with the disappointment and face a bad situation, hopefully wiser with a new strategy, and never give in to disappointment.

I mentioned earlier how I was denied housing even though I had a Ph.D. and earned a good living. Well, this is what happened.

I decided to move from a one-bedroom apartment to a seven-room apartment in an affluent part of Manhattan. When I presented myself to the owners of the building, who happened to be white, my application was denied. I later discovered that they just couldn't figure out why a single young black man would want a seven-room apartment. I think they thought I was renting the apartment to sell drugs—and I'm not talking Prozac, either. Yeah, I was angry, but I also wanted this Woody Allen-ish, long hallway, view of Riverside Park, huge apartment. So I put my anger aside and analyzed the problem. It wasn't that they didn't like me as a person, they just didn't know me. They probably didn't know any other black folks, either! So I called three psychologist friends of mine, who happened to be white, and had them write letters of reference. They stated something to the effect that "He's okay." A week later I was throwing my first party in my new seven-room apartment. As black folks, a lesson we must learn is that there is more than one way to skin a cat!

Be a role model to your child, especially in the way you handle adversity and racism. No matter the odds, show your child that you are strong, wise, graceful, and can forgive. No doubt, your child will develop the same strengths and character in dealing with life's injustices.

Solidarity among our race is all good but at the same time it is essential that you expand your kids' horizons by exposing them to children from other races and cultures. There are many benefits. Your children will get to personally experience how they are viewed by other races, especially whites. They will learn how to form strategies to fight prejudice based on experiences with the group. Most importantly, they learn not not fear interacting socially and professionally with people outside their race, and that's important.

The adage is true: If you want to win it, you've got to be in it.

The last piece of advice has to do with the emotional immune system. Just as the body's immune system fights disease, so can the emotional immune system (self-esteem) fight and protect the psyche from the ravages of racism. Therefore, you must build and strengthen you child's self-esteem through megadoses of emotional and spiritual vitamins. Every day recite with your child an affirmation or positive self-statement for the soul. The following eleven statements have become a blueprint for overcoming racism in my life. I hope they will inspire you and your child:

I am strong.
I eat adversity for breakfast.
I am equal to all.
I will succeed despite the odds.
I will break down all barriers placed before me.
I will not hate.
I will not forget, but I will learn and I will forgive.
I will work twice as hard if I am turned back the first time.
I will be an example for my people.
I will never give up.
I walk with God.

Ain't that the truth!

14

DR. JEFF ANSWERS PARENTS' QUESTIONS ON RAISING KIDS

WHETHER ON TALK SHOWS (including my own show, *Ask the Family Therapist* on America's Health Network), news shows, the street, or in one of my Rainbow clinics, I am always asked questions by frustrated parents, usually of color, on how to deal with various issues pertaining to raising their children. After over ten years of answering these questions in adverse situations, such as the time constraints imposed by television and radio, or even standing in the middle of a crowded subway approaching my stop, I have developed an expertise in assessing parents' issues and providing concise, commonsense strategies they can utilize to solve the problems they are experiencing with their children.

Over the years, I have recorded many of these questions with the hope that I would one day be sharing them with other parents who have similar problems or issues with their kids. I have taken some of the most popular questions I have been asked by parents and have provided practical and simple answers that you can easily use with your kids. I promise that my answers to your very important questions are tried, true, and keeping it *real*.

Q. My three-year-old does not like to make friends with other kids because he wants all of the toys for himself. What should I do?

A. All very young children are totally wrapped up in themselves. They view the universe as revolving around them. Therefore, they often have no interest and no capacity to share their toys with others. However, if this behavior continues into the ages of four and up, your child will be headed toward developing an antisocial personality. You must show your child that sharing can be an even more rewarding experience than playing alone. Try to arrange play dates or take him to the park to interact with other children. Provide positive reinforcement by praising him as much as possible when he does share and play with the other kids. He will slowly begin to learn that sharing is essential to make and keep friends. It is also part of growing more mature and, most important, bring smiles from mom and dad.

Q. *My four-year-old child is experiencing nightmares on a nightly basis. He is tired when he wakes up and cannot function in school. How do I get the nightmares to stop?*

A. Dreams and nightmares are classic signs that conflicts are being kept to oneself and not discussed with others, probably because they are too frightening. But the conflicts cannot be bottled up forever, and they seep out through nightmares while the child is sleeping and emotionally vulnerable. I suggest that you sit down with your child and find out what major issue is taking place that he is afraid to confront or talk about. Don't pressure him into speaking, but instead encourage anything he has to say, and keep communication open. This is going to be a work in progress, but eventually the whole story will come out. You will soon find that the nightmares will diminish, and he will get more restful sleep.

Q. *I'm trying to get my daughter to eat less sweets. However, when I deny her sweets she throws hissy fits. How do I handle this situation?*

A. Your question makes me think of the groups of black children who pass in front of my house every morning on the way to school. They are usually munching on their breakfast, which includes grape soda, Twinkies, and ice pops. Going into their first class, I bet you these kids are pumped up from sugar. By the second period, they are probably falling asleep after the sugar rush wears off. This kind of diet is very typical for black school-age children because of the abundance of junk food in the small candy stores and bodegas in so many black and Latino communities. It is only now that we are addressing the dietary issues of black children and their effects on their behavior and academic performance. As a matter of fact, many children with ADHD improved dramatically when sweets were eliminated from their diet. Therefore, I congratulate you and implore you to not to give up controlling your child's sugar intake.

One of the more effective strategies that you can utilize to control that sweet tooth is to set ground rules for eating sweets, such as:

- No sweets before a meal
- Only one sweet per day
- No sweets before bedtime
- No sweets if lunch or dinner are not eaten first
- Sweets given only as a reward (but not to bribe a child to keep quiet!)
- Substitute fruits for candies

One other thing: You must be consistent in following these rules or they will quickly become ineffective.

Because candy and other sweets are so pleasing to children, it will be difficult, even with rules, to keep them from gorging on them. Like your daughter, they will cry, threaten, and throw temper tantrums. And, quite often, we parents give in because we usually have no fight left in us ("give her the candy so she will stop whining"). But you know the old saying: you can pay now or pay later. In other words, don't give up. She will pluck your last nerve to get sweets, but if you persevere you will have a child who is physically and emotionally healthier, as well as being more academically successful. And isn't that the edge we want for our black children?

Q. Last month I enrolled my child for therapy services at the local community mental health center. When can I expect an improvement in his behavior? I'm also a little disappointed that they assigned him a white therapist. What can I do about that situation?

A. Most people do not understand that therapy is a very slow process in which the underlying reasons for the behaviors that are being addressed must be first brought to light. This normally takes some time because it is difficult to get a child to verbalize their issues. At the same time, the therapist must build a working and trusting partnership with the child in order to change short-term and, more importantly, long-term behaviors. Each case is different; therefore, I could not attempt to even give you an estimate of how long it would take for your child to get better. I can tell you it does not happen overnight, so you must be patient.

You can, however, speed up the process a little bit by becoming involved in the therapy. Before each session, give some brief information to the therapist about what's been happening with your kid. At the end of the session, speak with the therapist about any issues you should know. Sit in on sessions at least once a month so you can help explore issues from both you and your child's perspective. If the therapist is employing behavior modification techniques, make sure she teaches them to you so that you can continue this work with your child at home. Remember the old saying: You only get out of it what you put into it!

With regard to the situation of being assigned a white therapist, this is not automatically a bad situation. I have several white therapists who work at my Rainbow clinics. Because they are working primarily with black families and children, they have made it their business to become culturally sensitive and culturally competent in order to be effective with their clients. Be assertive and ask your child's therapist about her training and experiences in working with black children. If you sit in on the sessions as I suggested, you will know whether the therapist is effective with your child. If the "connection" is not there, it is your right to request another therapist and, this time, one of color.

Q. Dr. Gardere, I feel like a failure at times wondering where I went wrong with my six-your-old son, who is blatantly disrespectful to me. Is it too late to correct this problem, and if not, what can I do?

A. It is never, and I repeat, *never* too late to deal with any behavior problem, especially having to do with your child. You must remember that parenting is a work in progress. You will be parenting till you're dying day, because no matter how old your children get, you will always be the parent.

With regard to the respect issue, it has been my experience that children who lack respect for others usually lack respect for themselves. And since black children tend to have lower self-esteem on average, this is a particularly big problem in the African-American community. Over time they become bitter and hateful toward themselves and others. So it's quite simple. You must eliminate this bitterness by assisting your child in gaining respect for himself, as well as believing in his own abilities. Offer positive reinforcement and praise for anything he accomplishes. Constantly remind him that he is a beautiful and worthy black child who can accomplish anything in life. Always demonstrate love and compassion when dealing with him, and in time he will come to love himself and develop the capacity to treat others with warmth and respect.

Q. My seven-year-old is always crying. I think he may be depressed, but I'm not sure. Besides, I always thought depression was something that affects mostly affluent white children.

A. First off, black children actually suffer from depression at least as often as white children. The statistics may not have been available in the past to prove it, probably because of under-reporting procedures. However, the Centers for Disease Control recently reported that a higher percentage of black children are depressed and committing suicide as compared to white children. But looking at your specific case, there can be many possible causes for your child's crying. There might be something physical going on causing his depression, such as a hormonal imbalance or even a chemical imbalance in the brain. Of course, there might be a purely psychological depression related to some traumatic event. Get your child examined by a medical doctor to rule out any physical abnormalities. If that's all clear, you are looking at a psychological problem, probably depression. Think back on any situations that may have left your child extremely sad or fearful. Next, speak to him and try to engage him in brief conversations a few times a day with the goal of eliciting some conversation about whatever may be going on. Talking about the problem and allowing him to get it off his chest will go a long way in lifting the depression. At the same time, please be extremely aware of whether or not your child speaks of hurting himself or wanting to die. If he does, you should either get an emergency psychiatric evaluation or take the child to an emergency room for immediate treatment. At this point psychotherapy, or if the child is extremely young, play therapy, will be extremely helpful.

Q. My daughter has been holding in lots of anger due to her father's negligence in seeing her. She loves her stepfather very much, but she continues calling out for her biological father. What can I do?

A. Absent fathers are a continuing problem in the black community, posing unique problems for both sons and daughters. Boys in this situation tend to become undisciplined and unruly. However, daughters exhibit different psychological problems. They typically become angry when their biological fathers are not available, and many begin misbehaving both at school and at home. In addition, their relationships with males may begin to deteriorate, and the chances will increase that as they get older, they become involved in unstable and unhealthy liaisons with men.

The relationship a girl has with her father will serve as the blueprint she has with every male thereafter. I truly believe that this is part of the reason for the historical, conflicted relationships between black men and women. Therefore, the question is not what you can do, but more what can you and the biological father do, together, to address this problem. Even though the two of you are no longer together, you must team up to resolve this issue. The biological father is probably not aware that his daughter is suffering. Let him know what is going on. Find out what is keeping him away. It may be that he feels uncomfortable around you and your new husband. Discuss the issues and come up with solutions, together. Insist that he work out a schedule with you to visit and spend time with his daughter. Hold him accountable. Give him positive reinforcement such as verbal praise when he follows through. As his relationship with his daughter grows stronger, the love they will share will hopefully encourage him to visit more often and more willingly.

Q. *My nine-year-old niece was physically abused by her parents when she was three. She was removed by child protective services and placed in my home. Even though she has been living with us and away from her parents for the past six years, she still daydreams excessively, cries for no reason, and often has nightmares. What can I do to help her?*

A. Though you say many years have passed since she was abused, she may still be traumatized by the abuse, and is still experiencing the aftereffects. If you want to put a label on it, I would diagnose her as having posttraumatic stress syndrome (PTSD). PTSD occurs after someone has experienced a major traumatic event, such as physical abuse. They can experience anxiety, depression, flashbacks, and nightmares. I believe your niece is, in fact, experiencing all of these symptoms. This explains her crying spells, her daydreams (flashbacks), and of course her nightmares. I would recommend that your niece receive a psychological evaluation as quickly as possible to determine any other emotional issues, as well as any suicidal ideas related to her depression. In cases of PTSD, the preferred treatment is a combination of individual psychotherapy and medication to control anxiety and depression. There are also support groups that work with battered children. Call your local hospital to find out where and when these groups meet.

Finally, there are certain things that you and other family members can do on a daily basis to help your niece toward recovery. Be sensitive to her plight and show her plenty of love, but at the same time do not be condescending or make excuses for her behavior, for you will only further place her in the role of the outsider and victim. When the two of you are alone, or maybe even preparing a meal in the kitchen, get into some girl talk. Gauge her conversation about what happened with her parents in the past as well as how she feels about it presently. Talking is good. Getting problems off your chest can go a long way. And, of course, when you need to discipline her, whatever you do, do not ever use corporal punishment. This can be a disaster in light of the physical abuse she has experienced in the past. It would send her into a tailspin for sure. If you follow this advice, I really do believe your niece can overcome this tragedy and eventually move on to having a normal and healthy life.

Q. My nine-year-old child is hyper. He cannot read and no one can make out what he writes. He wanders outside of the class, constantly fighting. The public school is threatening to place him in special education. What do we do?

A. First of all, many black parents do not realize that children cannot be placed in special education without first being evaluated by a psychologist. Because of school budget cuts, there have been many situations in which kids have been placed in special education classes without proper or full evaluations. Therefore, request this evaluation as part of your child's rights, but even more importantly, because he really does need to be tested and treated.

It sounds like your child is experiencing some sort of learning disorder, as a result of or combined with attention deficit hyperactivity disorder. With these disorders there is a problem with the wiring of the brain, making the child unable to process information, pay attention, and remain calm. That is why there are problems with learning, being able to read, and general academic difficulties. As far as behavior is concerned, especially walking out of class and fighting, it has been my experience that black children usually have lower self-esteem than white children. The problems caused by the learning disorder or ADHD further lowers self-esteem because the child cannot keep up in class. Out of frustration the child becomes uninterested in class and becomes truant. His fighting is nothing more than the anger he experiences and acts out because he feels stupid.

After completing the evaluation, thoroughly discuss the results with the school-based evaluation and treatment team. They will offer suggestions on what type of class instruction and other supportive therapeutic services your child will need in order to begin learning properly. Supportive counseling will also be offered to allow your child the opportunity to express his frustrations. His self-esteem and related behaviors will soon improve, and you will once again have a normal, functioning child.

Q. My ten-year-old son sometimes gets so angry that he becomes violent and uses foul language. I'm so worried, I'm thinking of sending him to the military. How can I correct this problem and help my son control his temper?

A. There may be one of two situations taking place here. The first is that your son may have some legitimate reasons for being angry. Sit down with him and explore the issues he may have on his mind. Examine your own recent behavior, how you may have caused or contributed to his anger. Establish rules for your sit-downs, such as only allowing talking—no yelling or throwing of objects permitted. Above all, encourage and facilitate regular family communication so that anger and violence do not become the sole source of release.

The second situation, and the most common, may be based on the fact that anger and temper tantrums are a problem of impulse control (controlling emotions or behaviors) that develop very early in life due to the child always getting his way. In other words, your child may be spoiled. Being spoiled as a young child is tolerable, but remaining spoiled and being a brat at an older age is just plain ugly. As he gets older, his temper tantrums become more destructive and violent because he is naturally stronger. Since his language skills have also grown, he has more access to curse words, and as you have witnessed, he will use them to express frustration and anger when he does not get his way. You are right, this situation needs to be taken care of as quickly as possible. I don't think that the military should be the knee-jerk response. So many black parents see this as the first option to straighten out their kid. I would say that your son needs to be first "de-spoiled." If he continues along this path, I'm afraid it will lead to more antisocial behavior and even domestic violence after he is married. The last thing we need is another black man beating his wife!

Here's how you de-spoil him as quickly as possible. Both you and his father will need to establish discipline and set limits on outrageous and violent behavior. This means being extremely firm and not cutting him any slack when he throws his temper tantrums. Respond to any tantrum by placing him on a time-out and sending him to his room. If he begins to destroy his room, do not replace any items or clean up for him. Let him live in his mess; believe me, he'll stop trashing his room. Also, make it quite clear that foul language and raised voices will not be tolerated and will result in privileges being taken away. To help him get rid of some of that aggressive behavior, install a heavy bag (like the ones found in boxing gyms) in the basement. When he cannot control his anger, let him go a couple of rounds with the bag. This will dissipate his anger and allow him to deal with situations in a more calm and rational manner.

As with confronting any negative behavior, things will get worse before they get better. But hang in there; it's like riding the bunking bronco until it is tame; lots of spills, thrills, and danger!

Q. My eleven-year-old son's school just called to tell me he threatened to blow up the school and everyone in it. They are suspending him pending a psychological evaluation. I am angry and shocked that the school would react in this punitive manner. I'm also upset my son would make such a threat, even though I know he didn't really mean it and is just mouthing off as usual. I just don't know how to handle this situation.

A. This threat made by your son is extremely serious, whether he means it or not, especially in light of the children down South and in the Midwest who have gone on murderous rampages with guns and rifles. Even though these kids are white, do not be lulled into a false sense of security that it can't happen to your black child. The school is absolutely justified in suspending your son. You're really lucky that they didn't have him arrested. I think it's really a good idea that he receive a psychological evaluation in order to determine how real the threat is, and if nothing else, why he would make such a statement, even if not serious? Try to determine whether there was some precipitating factor at the school, such as a fight or disagreement with another student or teacher.

You really need to take a long hard look at what has been happening with your son lately. It seems to me that there is some bottled up rage beginning to come out that would cause him to make such a dangerous and inappropriate threat. Quite often, we as parents cannot accept that something may be seriously wrong in the household and tend to look the other way. Then the worst happens: a member of the family strikes out against themselves, family members, or others. These types of behaviors do not happen out of the blue; there are always indications. Whether or not your son meant the threats, they should be a wake-up call that something is drastically wrong. Sit your son down and find out what's bothering him. Determine what needs are being ignored that may be causing his rage. Have the family take responsibility for whatever part they contributed to the picture. Most importantly, constantly monitor what is going on with your son, what he does with his free time, and with whom he associates. I don't want to scare you, but the honest truth is that your son is at risk for explosive behavior. Stay on top of this and help your son heal his hate and hurt. P.S.: For all parents, but especially for this parent: If you have guns in the house, please get rid of them by turning them over to your local police precinct!

Q. *I can't understand why my preteen daughter insists on talking back to me all the time. It seems that she must always have the last word. What can I do to nip this annoying habit in the bud?*

A. As black parents we often feel that in order to show our authority we must have the last word. Sometimes parents are so strict with their children that talking back usually results in corporal punishment. These days the child who is rebellious will perceive such punishment as a challenge and will continue to talk back. What results is a contest of wills leading to escalating tension. Instead, you can show who is boss by discussing issues with your child in a calm and rational manner. Remember, the leader of the pack does not get ruffled and does not get baited into needless conversation. Speak softly and carry a big emotional stick. In other words, make your point and walk away. Your child can then continue to talk back, but only to himself, because you will no longer be in it. Believe me, after a while he'll get tired of talking to himself and will eventually stop back talking.

Q. *My son often complains that I don't listen to him and don't believe his side of the story. He feels that I often favor his brother and sister. How can I assure him that I do listen to him and will take his side, but only when he's right?*

A. What we may be looking at here is sibling rivalry. Your son is in competition with his brother and sister. Just keep drilling the message that you side with the person or sibling who is in the right. Everytime there is a situation involving the kids, point out your fairness and equal distribution of justice. Sometimes real examples are the best examples. If he still does not believe you after a while, then the problem may be deeper. He may also have basic problems with trust. Through various conversations, explore with your son where his problem of trust may have begun. Analyze and work on these issues by actively addressing and building a trusting relationship between the two of you that will serve as a model for his building trust with others.

Q. Whenever something happens, my thirteen-year-old daughter defends her actions by blaming someone else. Her favorite line is, "They started with me first." How can I help her take responsibility for her actions?

A. When I run into this situation with young clients or even my own kids, I tell them I can understand someone else starting trouble the first time. I can even understand someone else starting trouble the second time. But when it happens the third, fourth, or even the fifth time, there is a problem with avoiding responsibility for one's actions. That means it's time to get to work on addressing the problem.

You need to make it very clear to your child that she will not be allowed to cop out on anything or any situation. This means that even if she is not directly guilty of a certain infraction, she will still be held responsible for her actions and the actions of her friends. Besides, there are plenty of people who go to jail for being unwitting accomplices. If you are steadfast in this approach, your daughter will soon learn responsibility for her actions as well as accept responsibility for any situation in which she is involved. When you think about it, responsibility for one's actions is a life lesson and something we should all incorporate into our personalities in order to be successful in life.

Q. As a foster mom, I find my foster children are unable to express their feelings about being placed in foster care. How do I help them open up their communication skills?

A. Black children who have become part of the foster care system face many difficulties. For one, they suffer from the separation from their biological parents. Second, they are traumatized by whatever event got them placed into foster care, such as their parents' abuse of them. And with the epidemic of black kids in care, placements are often transitory. Many of these kids are placed in an at least three different foster homes before they are adopted or returned home. It is not uncommon for kids in this predicament to be very close mouthed about their situation. The bottom line is, they are having problems coping; that's what it's all about.

Because of all these issues, it is imperative that you encourage open communication with your foster kids by making their environment nonthreatening. One of the foster parents I work with has created what she calls "talk time." Every Friday evening at 7 P.M., she serves popcorn and juice and has her foster kids talk about whatever is troubling them. She has created a structured time for her kids to communicate their issues in a nonthreatening and fun manner. Give this a try. It should work for you and your foster kids.

Q. My fifteen-year-old daughter has turned from the sweetest little flower into a monster almost overnight. She is very disobedient, hangs out at all hours of the night with a bunch of bad-attitude kinds, and talks to me in a hateful manner. I'm at my wit's end and ready to put her out. What do I have to do to get my baby back?

A. It sounds to me like your daughter is out of control, especially if she is hanging with a rough crowd. It also seems that this outrageous behavior is out of character for her. She is acting out teen rebellion big time! No doubt the posse she has been hanging with has encouraged some of her negative behavior. Don't be surprised if she is experimenting with drugs and starting to have sex!

I think it's time for you to run to the nearest phone booth and change into Super Mom and take care of business. You're going to have to come in like gangbusters and retake control of your daughter and this situation before she ends up pregnant, on drugs, or worse. You must establish discipline by setting and enforcing curfews. Rules must be established that clearly define acceptable language and behavior toward parents and other authority figures. If your daughter violates any of the rules, punishments should include withholding privileges, as well as being grounded for a week at a time. Once you start tightening the screws the situation will get worse before it gets better, but it will get better.

I am concerned about her new friends and their negative influence. Get to know each and every one of these friends. Insist that they spend more time around your house, where you can keep an eye on their activities. Also get to know their parents so you can all strategize on how to deal with their rebellious behaviors.

Finally, establish a set time every day when you and your daughter can talk about the emotional issues of adolescence that she is dealing with, as well as just normal stuff. This will allow for a broadening of communication between the two of you. She will soon see that she can come to you to discuss any issue. She will also begin realizing that, at the end of the day, you, not her home boys and girls, are her best friend.

Q. I am continuously picking up and cleaning up behind my kids. How can I get them to clean their own rooms?

A. You are not alone with this problem. Most of the parents I have talked to complain that their kids are slobs. Most kids do not automatically pick up after themselves or clean their rooms; this is a habit that must be taught. This is a perfect opportunity for using positive reinforcement and the reward system. Begin by asking your kids to clean up after themselves and clean their rooms. Every time they do it well, make a really big deal about it by giving lots of verbal praise and perhaps rewarding them with extra dessert, or at the end of the month, with those Air Jordans they've been wanting. You can even have a contest whereby the person with the cleanest room over the period of one week gets the music or rap CD of their choice. If they don't keep their space tidy, they don't get the reward.

If you really want to get into guerrilla warfare, begin suspending privileges such as staying out late Friday night or getting on the Play Station after doing homework. When they are cut off from these earthly delights, they go into "addict" withdrawal. Make it clear that the only way they can get that fix is by making their beds and cleaning their rooms. I assure you, your kids will clean up after themselves if it means reinstating their rights to hang out at the rollerdrome!

Q. What do I say to my sixteen-year-old daughter who has been extremely rude to everyone in the house? To add insult to injury, she will strike up her Shaqueta *pose, you know, hands on hips, neck swinging, and declare she knows she is rude and will not change for anyone! How do I keep from slapping her down?*

A. Your daughter's behavior is what is known as defiance and resistance to authority figures. This rude behavior is primarily a way to get attention. You must understand, it's not that your kid is a bad child, it's just that like most kids, she does not know how to get parental approval in a constructive way, such as by doing good deeds or excelling in school. It seems that she has turned to rude or destructive behavior, which gets immediate parental attention, which results in more destructive behavior, which results in more parental attention. This is the classic vicious cycle. In order to break it, no matter what buttons your kid pushes, and it sounds like she knows how to push those buttons, do no overreact to negative or other rude behavior. But whatever you do, don't slap her, it only feeds into her attention-getting behavior.

In a calm manner, let her know that her present rude behavior is not acceptable. At all costs, avoid confrontation. She will soon understand that she will not receive attention for rude and confrontational behavior, and it will begin to diminish. Instead, go over the top by giving attention to only positive behavior, which will eventually increase.

Now, the second part of this puzzle is figuring out why your child is so desperate for your attention that she is willing to alienate everyone around her. It all goes back to establishing open communication. You must therefore establish an environment in which your child can talk to you about anything. Put time aside every single day when the two of you can sit down together and talk about what is happening in her life. Initially, you must be patient, allow for long periods of silence (due to initial resistance on her part), and be willing to listen more and lecture less. Knowing that she has your attention and support also will go a long way in diminishing her rude behavior. She simply won't need it anymore in order to get your attention.

Q. My husband died three months ago, and since that time my seventeen-year-old son refuses to talk about it. He stays in his room most of the time and has a hard time making friends. What do you think is going on?

A. It is very normal for your son and even other family members to react in this way, especially since the death of his dad is so recent. Your son is going through a bereavement process and is so sad and down that of course it is difficult for him to talk about his feelings. The best thing that you can do is give him his space to grieve by allowing him periods of privacy, especially when he is in his room.

At the same time, if he does not begin expressing his feelings to others, especially family members, he my become clinically depressed. It is important for your son and every member of the family, including yourself, to share your feelings and sadness over your husband's death through family meetings. Arrange for all the members of the household to gather in the living room or even over dinner to discuss their feelings of loss. If you can do this two to three times a week, you will be establishing an outlet for your son and other family members to express their grief in a positive manner, as well as keep your husband memory alive. Eventually, your son will go back to being his old self and will be able to reach out and establish new friendships and resurrect old ones. Again, the trick is to give him time to grieve but also keep him talking about his feelings and moving on with his life. It's a real balancing act, but with hard work and perseverance it can be accomplished.

APPENDIX: LIST OF SOCIAL SERVICE ORGANIZATIONS

(approved by the Partnership for a Drug-Free America)

African-American Family
  Services
2616 Nicollet Ave.
Minneapolis, MN 55408
(612)-871-7878

Al-Anon Family Group
  Headquarters, Inc.
1600 Corporate Landing Pkwy.
Virginia Beach, VA 23454
(757)-563-1600 (US)
(613)-722-1830 (Canada)

Alcoholics Anonymous World
  Services
475 Riverside Dr.
New York, NY 10115
(212)-870-3400

American Council for Drug
  Education
164 W. 74th St.
New York, NY 10023
(800)-488-DRUG

American Health Foundation
320 E. 43rd St.
New York, NY 10017
(212)-687-2339

Boys and Girls Clubs of America
1230 W. Peachtree St., NW
Atlanta, GA 30309
(404)-815-5700

Camp Fire, Inc.
4601 Madison Ave.
Kansas City, MO 64112
(816)-756-1950

CDC National Aids
  Clearinghouse
P.O. Box 6003
Rockville, MD 20849
(800)-458-5231

Center for Science in the Public
  Interest
1875 Connecticut Ave., NW, Suite
  300
Washington, DC 20009
(202)-332-9110

Center for Substance Abuse
  Prevention (CSAP)
Substance Abuse and Mental
  Health Services
  Administration
5600 Fishers Lane, Room 800
Rockville, MD 20857
(301)-443-0373
(800)-729-6686 (national clearing
  house)

Center for Substance Abuse
  Treatment (CSAT)
5600 Fishers Lane, Room 618
Rockville, MD 20857
(301)-443-5052

Clearinghouse on Family
  Violence Information
PO Box 1182
Washington, DC 20013
(800)-394-3366

Community Antidrug Coalitions
  of America (CADCA)
901 N. Pitt St. Suite 300
Alexandria, VA 22314
(703)-706-0560
(800)-54-CADCA

Drug Strategies
2445 M St., NW, Suite 480
Washington, DC 20037
(202)-663-6090

Families Anonymous
P.O. Box 3475
Culver City, CA 90231
(800)-7369805

Girls Incorporated
30 E. 33rd St., 7th Floor
New York, NY 10016
(317)-634-7546
(800)-374-4475

Hazelden Foundation
Box 11
Center City, MN 55012
(800)-328-9000

Join Together
441 Stuart St., 6th Floor
Boston, MA 02116
(617)-437-1500

"Just Say No" International
1777 N. California Blvd., Suite 210
Walnut Creek, CA 94596
(510)-939-6666
(800)-258-2766

Mothers Against Drunk Driving
  (MADD)
511 East John Carpenter
  Freeway, Suite 700

Irvington, TX 75062
(214)-744-6233
(800)-GET-MADD

Nar-Anon Family Groups
P.O. Box 2562
Palos Verdes Peninsula, CA
  90274
(213)-547-5800

Narcotics Anonymous
11426 Rockville Pike, Suite 100
Rockville, MD 20852
(301)-468-0985

National Association for
  Children of Alcoholics
11426 Rockville Pike, Suite 100
Seattle WA 98144
(206)-324-9360
(800)-322-5601

National Association for Native
  American Children of
  Alcoholics
611 12th Avenue South, Suite 200
Rockville, MD 20852
(301)-468-0985

National Black Child
  Development Institute
463 Rhode Island Ave., NW
Washington, DC 20005
(202)-387-1281
(800)-556-2234

National Center for Tobacco-Free
  Kids
1707 L St., NW, Suite 800
Washington, DC 296-5469
(800)-284-KIDS

National Clearinghouse for
  Alcohol and Drug Information
P.O. Box 2345
Rockville, MD 20847
(800)-SAY-NOTO

National Council on Alcoholism
and Drug Dependence, Inc.
12 W. 21st St., 7th Floor
New York, NY 10017
(212)-206-6770
(800)-NCA-CALL

National Crime Prevention
Council
1700 K Street, NW, 2nd Floor
Washington, DC 20006
(202)-466-6272
(800)-627-2911 (information
requests)

National Domestic Violence
Hotline
(800)-799-7233
Treatment facility referrals and
helpline
(800)-HELP-111
General reading list for parents

National Families in Action
2296 Henderson Mill Rd., Suite
300
Atlanta, GA 30345
(770)-934-6364

National Family Partnership
9220 S.W. Barbur Blvd., Nos.
119–284
Portland, OR 97219
Phone: (503) 5768-9659
Fax: (503) 244-5506

National Head Start Association
201 N. Union St., Suite 320
Alexandria, VA 22314
(703)-739-0875

National Inhalant Prevention
Coalition
1201 W. 6th St., Suite C-200
Austin, TX 78703
(800)-269-4237

National Institute on Drug
Abuse (NIDA)

5600 Fishers Lane, Room 10A03
Rockville, MD 20857
(301)-443-4577

National Urban League
Substance Abuse Program
500 E. 62nd St.
New York, NY 10021
(212)-310-9000

Office of Minority Health
Resource Center
P.O. Box 37337
Washington, DC 20013
(800)-444-6472

Office of National Drug Control
Policy (ONDCP)
P.O. Box 6000
Rockville, MD 20849
(800)-666-3332

Parents' Resource Institute for
Drug Education
50 Hurt Plaza, Suite 210
Atlanta, GA 30303
(404)-577-4500
(800)-853-7867

Safe and Drug-Free Schools
Program
U.S. Department of Education
1250 Maryland Ave., SW
Washington, DC 20024
(800)-624-0100

Students Against
Drunk Driving
200 Pleasant St.
Marlboro, MA 01752
(508)-481-3568

Toughlove
P.O. Box 1069
Doylestown, PA 18901
(215)-348-7090
(800)-333-1069
www.toughlove.org

BIBLIOGRAPHY

"AIDS Among Racial/Ethnic Minorities—United States, 1993." *Morbidity and Mortality Weekly Report* 43, no. 35 (1994).

Amnesty International, "USA Police Brutality Widespread Problem in New York City." June 26, 1996.

Axelrod, Lauren, *TV Proof Your Kids*. New Jersey: Citadel Press, 1997.

Bauman, Lawrence. *The Ten Most Troublesome Teenage Problems and How to Solve Them*. New Jersey: Citadel Press, 1986.

Begley, Sharon. "The Parent Trap." *Newsweek*, September 7, 1998.

Bench, R. J. and Anderson, J. H., "Sound Transmission to the Human Fetus Through the Maternal Abdominal Wall." *Journal of Genetic Psychology* 113 (1968): 85–87.

Brody, Jane. "Mary S. Calderone, Advocate of Sexual Education, Dies at 94." *New York Times*, October 25, 1998.

Bronner, Ethan. "Fewer Minorities Entering U of California." *New York Times*, May 21, 1998.

Cose, Ellen. "Rage of the Privileged." *Newsweek*, November 15, 1993.

Dodd, Vikram. "Chief Constable Admits Police Display Institutional Racism." *New York Observer*, August 9, 1998.

Eisenberg, Arlene, et al. *What to Eat When You're Expecting*. New York: Workman Press, 1986.

Fremon, Celeste, and Hamilton, Stephanie Renfrow. "Are Schools Failing Black Boys?" *Parenting*, 1994.

Gay, K. B., and Goulding, Sexon. "Medical Correlates of High-Risk Maternal Behavior in Babies Born to Cocaine-Abusing Mothers." *Pediatric Research* 27, no. 243A (1990).

Gest, Emily, and Dave Saltonstall. "Parents Are Back in Style." *New York City News*, April 27, 1998.

Heniz-Erian, Peter, and Spitzmuller, Andrea. "Maternal Smoking and Inhibition of Fetal Growth Factor." *Journal of the American Medical Association* 279, no. 24 (1998).

Holt, Karen. "Parents Look Past Drugs for Attention Disorders." *Westchester Herald Statesman*, June 16, 1998.

Hutchinson, Earl. "Why Are More Black Young Men Killing Themselves?" *New York Beacon*, June 4, 1998.

Jaroff, Leon. "Teaching Reverse Racism." *Time*, April 4, 1994.

Johnson, Robert. *Mayo Clinic Complete Book of Pregnancy and Baby's First Year.* New York: William Morrow, 1994.

Jordan Sandra. *Yoga for Pregnancy: Safe and Gentle Stretches.* New York: St. Martin's Press, 1988.

Kifner, John, and Herszenhorn, David. "Racial 'Profiling' at Crux of Inquiry Into Shooting by Troopers." *New York Times*, May 8, 1998.

Leland, John. "Savior of the Streets." *Newsweek*, June 1, 1998.

Leland, John, and Samuels, Allison. "Generation Gap." *Newsweek*, March 17, 1997.

Lemonick, Michael. "Spare the Rod? Maybe." *Time*, August 25, 1997.

Lewin, Tamar. "One in Eight Boys of High School Age Has Been Abused, Survey Shows." *New York Times*, June 26, 1998.

Lewin, Tamar. "Public Schools Confronting Issue of Racial Preferences," *New York Times*, November 29, 1998.

Males, Mike. "Five Myths, and Why Adults Believe They Are True." *New York Times*, April 29, 1998.

Marwick, Charles. "Leaving Concert Hall for Clinic, Therapists Now Test Music's Charms." *Journal of the American Medical Association* 24, no. 31 (1996).

McGrath, Judy. "Youth Views Towards Sex and AIDS." *Muscle and Fitness*, July 1998.

Meier, Barry. "Disputed Statistics Fuel Politics in Youth Smoking." *New York Times*, May 20, 1998.

National Campaign to Prevent Teen Pregnancy. "Whatever Happened to Childhood? The Problem of Teen Pregnancy in the United States." Washington, D.C., 1997.

Raab, Selwyn. "Queens Jury Spares Convicted Killer From Death Penalty." *New York Times*, December 19, 1998.

Revkin, Andrew. "Herbal Tobacco Substitutes on Rise and So Are Worries." *New York Times*, May 24, 1998.

Rhode, David. "Despite Deal, Family of Man Who Died in Arrest Assails Mayor." *New York Times*, October 3, 1998.

Rosenbaum, David. "New Attack on Cigarette Makers." *New York Times*, June 29, 1998.

Samalin, Nancy, and Whitney, Catherine. "What's Wrong With Spanking?" *Parents*, May 1995.

"Spanking Makes Children Violent, Antisocial." *American Medical Association News Update*, August 13, 1997.

Stodghill, Ron. "Where'd You Learn That?" *Time*, June 15, 1998.

Straus, Murray. *Beating the Devil out of Them: Corporal Punishment in American Families.* New York: Lexington Books, 1995.

"Syphilis Rate Plummets by 84 Percent in the 90s." *New York Times,* June 25, 1998.

"Teenage Drug Use on the Rise, New Government Survey Reports." *New York Times,* August 21, 1998.

Tupler, Julie, and Thompson, Andrea. *Maternal Fitness: Preparing for Healthy Pregnancy.* New York: Simon and Schuster, 1996.

U.S. Department of Education. *Growing Up Drug Free: A Parents Guide to Prevention.* Washington, D.C., 1997.

U.S. Department of Health and Human Services. "Race/Ethnicity of Children Entering Foster Care." Washington, D.C., 1996.

Wakschlag, Lauren, et al. "Maternal Smoking During Pregnancy and the Risk of Conduct Disorder in Boys." *Archives of General Psychiatry* 54 (1997): 670–76.

Williams, Monte. "Irate Rappers Give Journalist a Combat Beat," *New York Times,* December 22, 1998.

"Youth Smoking Rises 83 Percent in Nine Years." *New York Times,* October 8, 1998.

INDEX